A GARDENER'S GUIDE TO

GARDENING ON A GRADIENT

Designing and Establishing Sloping Gardens

A GARDENER'S GUIDE TO

GARDENING ON A GRADIENT

Designing and Establishing Sloping Gardens

CAROL SMITH

THE CROWOOD PRESS

First published in 2022 by
The Crowood Press Ltd
Ramsbury, Marlborough
Wiltshire SN8 2HR

enquiries@crowood.com

www.crowood.com

British Library Cataloguing-in-Publication Data
A catalogue record for this book is available from the British Library.

ISBN 978 0 7198 4086 5

Image credit
K Quinn Ferris, Dreamstime.com, (p.77) top.

Typeset and designed by Jean Cussons Typesetting, Diss, Norfolk
Cover design by Blue Sunflower Creative
Printed and bound in India by Parksons Graphics

CONTENTS

DEDICATION

In 2011 my first book, *Designing Gardens with Plant Shapes*, was dedicated to our first grandchild, Lily Mia. We now have a second grandchild, a boy named Maxwell, so it seems fitting to dedicate this, my second book, to Max.

ACKNOWLEDGEMENTS

I would like to thank everyone for their unfailing encouragement when I was writing this second book. Aimed at all gardeners, from keen beginners to students to professionals, it has been born out of personal experience and my lecturing days.

First, to Colin, my wonderful husband and closest friend, whose constant support is second to none; his numerous cups of tea have kept me going! His encouragement, patience and unfailing belief in me have been constant throughout the last twelve months as I wrote the book. My great son Kevin for his continued interest in my progress even though working on a PhD himself. My amazing daughter Sharon is incredibly busy with two children and working full-time, but always finds the time to ring, and often remotivates me when the going has been challenging.

My dear friends Sue Evans, Tina Williams, Diane Elt, Joy Beech, Amy Stone and Sharon Minchin have for many years lent an ear to my ideas and encouraged me in my desire to write about my passion for plants and gardens.

Thank you all.

INTRODUCTION

A sloping garden will present any gardener with a challenge that can seem rather intimidating, and even overwhelming. What on earth can you do with it? Where do you start? Even a professional might find themselves puzzling over the same questions, but at least they will be able to draw on experience and technical knowledge. However, although this type of site may be a difficult proposition, demanding additional time, assessment and forward planning, the end results will be well worth the extra effort required.

Whatever level you are working at, certain factors will reduce the options open to you, and it is fair to say that budget is at the top of the list of these factors. Broadly speaking, all the initial decisions that will need to be made will be influenced by the amount of money available for the project. These include the choice of whether to approach the development from a 'construction' perspective, usually involving the costly building of steps and retaining structures, or to adopt the more cost-effective option of remodelling the site by undertaking 'earthworks'. That is not to say that the earthworks approach cannot include steps; of course it can. Indeed, it may be the case that, due to a greater percentage of the work being less costly 'soft' works, adding steps of hard materials becomes affordable. And, by using natural materials such as tree bark for the treads and natural timbers for the risers, such hard landscaping structures can become even more cost-effective. All these options will be explored in Chapter 4.

Chapters 1 to 5 look at all aspects of the pre-build stage, the aim being to take the reader through the process, so that they have a strong structure that can be applied to the development of any sloping garden. Details are given in step-by-step stages regarding the assessment and recording of both existing and proposed site levels, progressing into the ways in which the levels will inform design choices and planning: the number and position of steps, the height of retaining structures, the proportions of hard or soft landscaping. Most of the descriptions are diagrammatic, with explanatory text. They also encompass drawing techniques with supporting text, providing a visual means by which all aspects of the sloping site can be assessed and all options for improving it can be shown.

Chapters 6 to 8 focus on the planting and soft landscaping aspects, the effect on decision-making of working with a slope, and why it is important to identify site specifics such as aspect, drainage and soil characteristics. Due attention needs to be paid to all of these, as they will have a radical impact on the success or otherwise of the sloping garden. Planting design considerations and options, including the most appropriate plant groups for plant choices, are all explored in detail, in the form of a small plant library with images and explanatory text.

Having worked on many sloping garden sites, both large and small, during my career as a garden designer, I know only too well the challenges that they present. Not least of these is the difficulty of obtaining reliable information. The advice available on working through this particular challenge is very disparate and fragmented – and much of it is conflicting, anyway. Time-consuming multiple website visits, reading and searching to discover the few paragraphs dedicated to the subject in books and magazines, are not only frustrating, but also incredibly laborious when you just want to get on with the job in hand. That pile of notes on website shortcuts, books and articles covering your desk will lack cohesion, cause confusion and fail to give you a clear way forward.

The main goal of this book is to provide anybody facing the challenge of a sloping site with a concise, detailed, easily read and understood handbook, which as far as possible covers the questions, uncertainties and confusion they may have. Informative text, logical procedures, diagrams and images aim to provide the reader with all they need to tackle the challenge with inspiration and confidence. The final result should be the creation of a sloping garden that is safe, easy to access and enjoyable to move around. It will not only look beautiful but will have been a pleasure to develop.

CHAPTER 1

SLOPES AND LEVELS: ANALYSIS AND OPTIONS

From the flat plains of Norfolk to the undulating, mountainous peaks of the Lake District, the UK is a land of extremely varied levels; as a result, many a gardener will find themselves having to deal with a sloping site. This varied terrain presents all sorts of interesting challenges in terms of leisure pursuits, both at home and away. In the broader landscape, it can provide a place for exciting experiences such as hill walking, abseiling and

Fig. 1.1 A sloping front garden before development…

Fig. 1.2 ...and after.

climbing, for relaxation and exercise. Closer to home, the smaller landscape – your own piece of green space – offers the opportunity to participate in, and take great satisfaction from, another outdoor activity: gardening!

Some gardeners love to indulge in an unspoken rivalry through the summer months, partaking with their neighbours in the 'perfect lawn' competition. They may go to great lengths to achieve the neatest stretch of grass, complete with stripes. However, it is fair to say that a completely flat garden, even one with an impressive lawn, can lack interest – it can even be a bit boring. When the whole garden can be seen all at once, there is no 'draw' and therefore no need to explore it further, to satisfy the observer's natural sense of adventure. Introducing changes of level and division to a flat garden will increase the visual interest, creating a desire to take a journey into and around the garden, to enjoy the adventure. It is not dissimilar to the ways in which an artist will use perspective, colour, light and shade to draw the viewer into a picture.

Gardening on a slope will always demand some level of intervention to improve its function. There will be a cost involved, but the impact of this will be offset by the bonus of greatly increased 'kerb appeal' and usability. For example, when steps are designed with more than simply function and essential safety in mind, they can provide a significant amount of interest. One source of inspiration might be an amphitheatre, which has a high visual impact, with its strong, dynamic curves and gently ascending levels. It would of course be impossible to have such a large structure in an average garden, but the general idea can be scaled down to fit, resulting in both a retaining structure and steps at the same time (*see* Fig. 1.3). The steps with cushions on them can provide additional seating for outdoor entertaining, and form a retaining structure that is much more attractive than a plain brick or block wall would be. A plain wall would not only look harsh, but also create a strong sense of division, whereas the curving steps link the upper and lower levels together in a much softer, more appealing way.

A sloping garden will require even more time and thought than a flat garden. First, there will need to be detailed consideration of the practicalities, such as where steps and flat areas will be best placed. Second, you will need to look at the design opportunities that are open to you, and which can make a huge improvement, raising the garden's visual interest and injecting

Fig. 1.3 Steps in the style of an amphitheatre.

Fig. 1.4 Steps with a landing mid-flight.

the wow factor. It is an undeniable fact that a sloping garden will require investment, so why not make the most of the opportunity to create a beautiful garden, rather than one in which you regret the things you did not do?

There are a number of advantages and disadvantages to the sloping garden. It is great to adopt a constructive and positive approach to developing such a site, but it is equally important to recognize the potential disadvantages.

Potential Disadvantages

- The gradient: how steep or complicated is the gradient, and does it run in different directions? Particular thought will need to be given to the design if it slopes towards a neighbouring property; how will water run-off will be kept within the confines of the boundaries?
- Cost: is it a project that needs professional input in the form of a garden designer, landscape architect, structural engineer or contractor? If it does, this will be more expensive, but the additional costs will be worthwhile if it helps you to achieve a safe, functional outcome.
- Slope direction – towards the property: the direction of the slope will have a bearing on the drainage aspects of the development. For example, there may be a need for a drainage system around the house perimeter. Such a system may have already been installed, usually in the form of a gravel-filled channel. Alternatively, drainage may be required next to a path or patio at the base of a slope to prevent run-off on to the surface. Hard surfaces are usually found directly outside the house and need to be kept frost-free and non-slippery during the winter months.
- Shade: frost and ice are not the only slip hazards. A hard surface that lies in shade, whether because of the direction in which it faces, or because of overhanging tree branches, fencing and walls, will often remain damp and become slippery due to an algal growth on the surface.
- Slope direction – away from the property: if this is the case, much of the garden will not be seen from the house unless the terrain is remodelled to raise its level.

Fig. 1.5 The surrounding sloping land all runs down to the lowest point in front of the tree.

Advantages

- Additional height: mounded earth, with the addition of strategically placed trees, can be used to block an undesirable view or, conversely, to maximize a favourable view.
- Increased visual impact: can be achieved by terracing or re-contouring the slope. Natural contours give an exceptionally soft, visually relaxing effect and raised mounds can also be utilized to create distinct areas within the garden.
- Higher viewpoints: different levels can allow for the creation of a raised deck area for relaxation and dining, overlooking a lower lawn area for games or providing a new viewpoint on to a particularly beautiful planting scheme.
- Natural vantage points: a slope can offer the opportunity to create vantage points both in the garden and beyond, providing perfect sitting areas.
- A sense of enclosure and privacy: this will prevail if the slope is towards the house, with all of the garden being seen from the lower viewpoint of the property. On the other hand, where a garden is sloping away from the house, less attractive features such as a shed can be hidden out of sight.
- A sense of intrigue and adventure: the observer will be drawn to explore if the slope is away from the house, to discover what is beyond and can be seen.
- Inclusion of high-impact features: the slope may provide an opportunity to include features such as water cascades. These are especially effective in a sloping garden – not only are they visually impressive, they can also help with drainage, an important consideration if a sloping garden is to function effectively.

The Design Process: Site Analysis

In order to establish a strong starting point, the first key to designing and planning a garden, and more importantly a sloping garden, is an assessment of the site. The aim is to establish the difference between the highest and lowest points of the garden. There may be more than one highest and lowest point if the slope runs in different directions, but this is not a common occurrence. This may sound like an oversimplification, but all will become clear in Chapter 3, where the technique of section drawing will be demonstrated. This is the base from which everything else will evolve – once you can see the slope and measure the difference between the highest and lowest points drawn to scale, you can progress on to calculating the height of the retaining structures, the number of steps required, or the proposed height of a single mound or several mounds of varying heights. With a thorough assessment early on, planning the development becomes a much easier task.

The second key to designing a garden is to adopt a structured, planned approach, in which the task is broken down into 'bite-sized' stages, making the whole process feel much more accessible. The site analysis is the first stage. There are many factors to be considered and taking the time to don your boots and coat, and grab your notebook, pencil and camera to go out and create a checklist is a constructive way to begin the task ahead.

The site analysis involves making detailed observations and recording them as notes, with supporting photographs. Once you are back at your desk, the next step is to set up the photos and notes as a Word or Publisher doc on a PC or stick the pictures in a notebook and write observations alongside each one. This will give you a visual description of what you have observed around the site. Your notes might read as follows: 'existing slope is too steep to walk comfortably, existing steps are in poor condition, slope is south-facing', and so on. Once you have built up a detailed analysis, your observations will underpin design decisions that will be taken when you reach that stage in the project.

You will also need to carry out a levels survey to add to the site analysis. The method for doing this will be covered in Chapter 3.

While you are working through the process of analysing the site, you may find that ideas start to emerge. These can be recorded alongside your pictures. The challenges of a sloping site may lead you to consider all sorts of interesting concepts that would not occur to you when working on a flat site. The changes of level will enable the creation of a more visually dynamic composition and open up many possibilities, such as terracing, water cascades, raised beds instead of walls, and seating areas on different levels to maximize views, to name just a few. Improving functionality

Fig. 1.6 A site analysis sheet.

and safety are the main aims when developing a sloping garden. For example, a flight of steps may be provided with 'landings', to give resting points at certain intervals, making it less taxing than walking up a steep slope without steps (*see* Fig. 1.4).

The surface of the slope is of paramount importance when considering safety. If it is of grass or bare soil, there are potential slip and erosion issues. Both these issues can be mitigated by decreasing the gradient to a gentle slope. A slope may not be so steep that it requires this particular treatment – it may be shallow, or somewhere between the two – yet it will still need to be remodelled, perhaps by splitting the levels in order to provide a flat surface for tables, chairs, and other garden structures.

When doing your site analysis, your checklist should include the following (take photographs of each observation as you work around the site):

- In which direction does the slope run – towards or away from the property, or in more than one direction? These variables offer different design opportunities and require different management of the garden development.
- Are there signs of run-off? There may be evidence of this in the form of a soil sediment line at the base

of the slope. It suggests that soil erosion is occurring due to the two factors of the soil type and the gradient of the slope, and is a strong indicator that retaining structures or a soil stabilization method will be required.

- On a scale of 1 to 10, how steep or shallow is the slope? (Instructions on how to calculate this accurately can be found in Chapter 3.)
- Are there any existing steps and/or retaining structures such as walls? Measuring the total height of these can be used to give a rough overall change of level.
- What is the access to the site like? Is it affected by the slope, and if so, how? Is the access up or down the slope? This will influence material choices particularly to ensure safe winter weather use.
- What is the aspect of the site? This will affect the levels of sun and shade in the garden. For example, an east-facing slope or garden will have less sun, especially in the evening.
- Is there enough flat space around the property? If not, then excavation will need to be carried out to increase the capacity for pathways and patio areas. If the slope is running away from the property, a method called 'cut and fill' can be used to create flat areas; there is more detail on this in Chapter 3.
- How is the garden to be used? The answer to this question will depend upon the taste and situation of the owner. They may be a single older person, or a younger one, they may have a family or they may be a couple without children. Almost every type of owner will appreciate a flat area outside the house, either at the front or the back, or both, depending on where the slope is. This area could be used for entertainment or for simply sitting out with a cup of tea, or to provide a level area by an entrance door. A garden that is being designed for a family, for example, is likely to require a flat lawn area for children's games and activities.
- Approximately, where are any structures to be sited?
- Will the garden need a ramp or ramps, as well as steps? This would be the case if the garden is to be used by an elderly or disabled person.
- What is the budget?

Design Options and Budget

It is exciting at the beginning of a garden project, when you start to explore the possibilities and consider exactly what it is that you want, and where it is going to be. When designing or planning any garden, efficient and safe functionality is a major goal and this becomes even more of a priority in the case of a sloping garden. The final positions of a patio, an entertainment area and the more functional parts of any garden all require careful planning and consideration. A patio at the bottom of a slope, for example, a long walk from the kitchen or barbecue area, will not be practical – not least because your food may be cold by the time it gets to the table!

The time you spend making decisions about whether to include a summerhouse, pergola or arbour, high-impact features such as a fountain or cascade, exciting large steps, expansive planting, or innovative use of materials, can be short-circuited by drawing up a wish list before you even start to think about where to position them and what they are to be made from. However, before you get carried away with all these exciting ideas, your first priority when working with a sloping site is to get the 'bones' of the garden right. This means making carefully considered decisions on the positioning of level areas and steps, and working out how they will link with each other, enabling easy access to and from one to the other, and allowing for an easier journey around the garden and up and down the slope.

The design possibilities open to you will be strongly influenced by the budget that is available – inevitably, the bigger the budget, the greater the number of design opportunities. With a more generous budget, you may be able to incorporate retaining structures and terraces made of more costly hard materials, such as slabs, brick, block, stone and sleepers. Such structures often appear on a gardener's wish list, but their inclusion can only become a reality if there is enough money available. They involve extra costs in terms of labour and the engagement of a skilled contractor to install them, and sometimes also need more work in the form of a drainage system. In terms of design and the finished look, this type of development will give a more formal appearance to the garden, but this can be softened with planting, particularly in the vicinity of the hard faces of the retaining structures.

If the budget available is less generous, or you have a personal preference to create a more 'naturalistic' style to the development, your best way forward may be via the creation of modified slopes, otherwise known as 'earthworks'. In this case, the greater proportion of the budget will be absorbed by the costs of an operator on a digger moving earth around to create mounds and undulations that will reduce the gradient of the slope. Finished with a grass surface, or a combination of grass and large drifts of loose planting, these can look really beautiful. They will be low-maintenance and reduce the need for expensive drainage systems. In addition, they provide an environmentally healthy green space, with wildlife-friendly micro habitats. There are many reasons why this type of development is currently extremely popular.

Most projects that involve a significant amount of construction, whether it is to be done by a contractor or by a self-builder, will need to be scheduled for the months of the year when the weather is expected to be better. If time is lost on a late summer/early autumn project, delaying it until later into the year, when the weather is less reliable, the work will probably be pushed over into the following spring. Most contractors will not lay slabs or build walls requiring the use of mortar if there is any risk of excessive wet and/or frost. Delays can prove to be costly, particularly where a contractor has been engaged and has no other project to move on to, and the gar- den owner is suffering the inconvenience and mess of months of muddy boots and machinery. Which- ever approach is being followed – hard landscaping or earthworks – it is important to use the site analysis and assessment to identify any potential delays and difficulties that might occur later on.Factoring in and resolving any increased costs at an early stage can help to prevent undue worry and frustration.

CHAPTER 2

CREATING A BRIEF

One of the main aims when designing and planning a garden should be to resolve any structural and aesthetic problems in an existing layout or a new site. Undertaking a proper assessment and analysis, and drawing up a detailed brief, may seem laborious and time-consuming, but it is the only way to achieve the eventual desired outcome of a safe, attractive and manageable sloping garden. Taking this approach, and creating a clear and concise brief, is a productive and valuable use of your time. Hopefully it will prevent any misunder-

Fig. 2.1 A garden that had a slope from right to left.

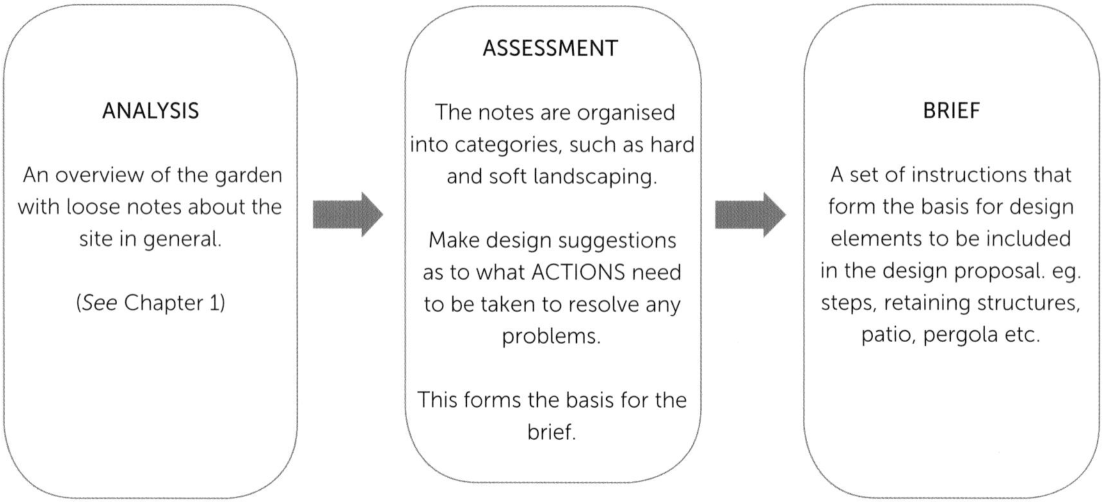

Fig. 2.2 The order of the tasks to be undertaken.

standings or unplanned costs during the development of the project.

Take plenty of time to walk around the site, making your way up and down the slope or slopes. This will give you a 'live' experience, in which any problems or issues will soon become apparent, enabling you to clarify decisions regarding the future placement of flat areas, steps, ramps and retaining structures. The end goal is to facilitate the efficient and safe use of the garden, creating an outdoor space that is enjoyable and easily maintained. In order to achieve this goal, you will need to take time to become familiar with both the desirable and less desirable aspects of the site.

Gathering Information for a Brief

At the very beginning of a garden project, whether you are designing for a client or for your own back garden, it is important to have a clear idea not just of what needs to be done to prepare the garden for its transformation, but also of exactly how the final garden is to look. There are certain tasks, such as drawing up a brief, which need to be completed in order to arrive at the final destination. Once you have a clear brief,you can move forward into the planning and layout stages.

When you are undertaking your assessment, it is useful to note down the information that you gather as an 'Observation', followed by the necessary or desired 'Instruction/Action'.

Hard Landscape Considerations

If there are any existing elements of hard landscaping that are in poor condition, such as patios, steps and walls, they will need to be removed, replaced or repositioned to improve the function and aesthetics of the garden. Any such elements should be noted in your assessment in a way that first describes their existing condition and then gives an instruction on how to deal with them. For example, your initial notes might look like the following:

Flat surfaces

Observation: Existing patio is uneven, mortar joints are collapsing and full of moss.

Instruction/Action: Needs to be removed and replaced.

Retainers

Observation: Existing wall is leaning, faces are coming off the bricks, shows signs of severe disintegration.

Instruction/Action: Needs to be removed. Install new retainer.

Structures

Observation: Old timber shed [pergola, summerhouse, and so on] is rotten.
Instruction/Action: To be removed and replaced. [If the structure is to be reused and moved to a new position, make a note to this effect.]

Fencing

Observation: Most of the fencing is rotten and unstable.
Instruction/Action: Needs to be repaired [or removed and replaced].

These notes and comments on the functionality of existing hard garden elements will inform and enable the development of a number of lists: tasks that need to be done ('site preparation'); elements that need to be repaired or replaced; and new elements to be included in the design proposal.

Among all of the information gathering and list-making, it is important not to lose track of the overall aim of the evaluation of a sloping site: to assess the level of difficulty of access posed by the existing slope.

Soft Landscape Considerations

Remedial work to existing plants is inevitable on any garden project. It usually takes the form of pruning or reshaping but, in the worst case scenario, removal may be necessary. Photos of the plants that require work can be included in the assessment as a visual reminder. Combined with written notes, these will make the formulation of a comprehensive plan for this aspect of site preparation much easier. The clearest way to organize the information is to divide it into appropriate plant groups, such as trees and shrubs. Notes can then be made of any work needed to specific specimens and on the location of any new plants that are to be included. The notes can also cover detail such as whether an evergreen or ornamental plant is required, eventually building up a plant list that can be returned to later.

Trees

The services of an arboriculturist may be required, to inspect and assess the condition and stability of any mature trees. It is wise to seek this advice to prevent future problems in the garden being developed or in a neighbouring garden. A variety of work may be required:

- Radical pruning to prevent branch breakages.
- Raising the crown to reduce shade from overhanging branches.
- Pruning to regenerate new growth.

A difficult decision may need to be made if there is a diseased tree in poor condition. If it is necessary to have it removed, it may be a sad day, but it will give you the opportunity to plant another tree, or even several new ones.

Shrubs

Once you have assessed the shape, location and condition of all the shrubs in the garden, you can draw up a list of the work that may be required:

- Cutting back of mature specimens, to shape the plants and stimulate new growth.
- Hard pruning, also known as remedial pruning, to ensure future health and new growth, and a flourish of blooms in season.
- In some cases, removal of seriously overgrown shrubs, to create space and improve air circulation.

Of course, this type of work must be done in the right season. For example, if a spring-flowering shrub is pruned in autumn, it will not flower the following spring as all the forming buds will have been removed.

Weeds

Although the cultivation of weeds does not really count as soft landscaping, it is important to factor in any work that may be required to deal with perennials such as ground elder, nettles, bramble and convolvulus on the site.

Chemical weedkiller is the treatment of choice for speedy and long-lasting results (although it can take several weeks). Many people are opposed to using chemicals for a variety of reasons, but most modern treatments become inert once they make contact with the soil. Indeed, the chemical approach is often the only option for areas that have been neglected for many years.

If time is not an issue, a chemical-free method can be used. This involves covering the weedy area with black plastic and leaving it for several months, starving the weeds of daylight and oxygen, so that they die. This method is lengthy, however, requiring a period of several weeks after the removal of the plastic, during which the ground must be observed for any signs of regrowth. To ensure that all the weeds have died, and the ground is completely clear, it may need to be repeated several times. Convolvulus, ground elder and bramble are notoriously difficult to clear, as their spaghetti-like roots can go down several feet into the soil. Taking this into consideration, you may decide that the chemical approach is the most time-efficient and reliable.

Drainage and Soil

On your walk around the garden, you need to look out for evidence of poor drainage or any issues with the soil:

- Soft, boggy ground with shallow surface puddling indicates a problem with drainage.
- A spongy, mossy lawn can also be the result of poor drainage.
- A nasty odour of stagnant water can occur where the ground has become anaerobic. In other words, waterlogging has caused the water to become stale, with no oxygen. Plants will be dead or extremely sick.

Fig. 2.4 A French drain.

Fig. 2.3 Waterlogged soil. Note the lie of the land to this low point.

- If the soil is sticky clay, it will fail to absorb or allow surface water to drain away and so become waterlogged, depriving the plants of oxygen and causing the roots to rot.

The importance of these observations of the soil is usually self-evident. Less obvious is the need to recognize the 'lie of the land' around the site, by really looking carefully at its slope directions. Identifying this will tell you how boggy the soil gets and where the water is coming from (*see* Fig. 2.3).

For example, where the surrounding land slopes towards the centre of the site, any storm water will drain into the garden. This can be improved by the installation of a French drain system – basically a trench with slotted pipes in its base, back-filled with gravel. The base of the trench is dug to slope away from the garden, to take any water away via the pipes. If there are large quantities of water involved, a collection point known as a soakaway will also need to be installed.

Fig. 2.5 An ACO channel.

Fig. 2.6 A wall with weep holes.

Do's and Dont's for Drainage

Do's

Use non-slip surfaces for any flat areas at the bottom of the slope.

Position a lawn where it will get at least 8 hours' sunlight per day. On clay soil, intensive soil prep will be needed to improve drainage.

Terrace/split-level the slope wherever possible to reduce the amount of water reaching the bottom of the slope.

Install an ACO or gravel channel to run along the base of any retaining structures to collect run-off before it reaches the bottom of the slope.

Don'ts

If run-off water is allowed to flow on to a walking surface in shade, it will become slippery with algae.

On clay soil, a lawn at the base of a slope will always have moss and will struggle to grow successfully.

Weep holes should not drain on to a walking surface. If in shade, algal growth will thrive, and in winter run-off can freeze – both will result in a slip hazard.

Any planting areas will need intensive soil prep to improve growing conditions for new plants, reduce ongoing maintenance and optimize soil condition.

Planting

The planting is the final – and perhaps the most vital – layer of the garden. Adding plants is like putting the icing on a cake. It is what softens and transforms the hard elements to make a real garden, pulling it all together and creating a living outdoor space that is vibrant with colour, shape and life. Often, bees and butterflies will arrive in a garden within a couple of hours of the plants being put in – it is such a pleasing phenomenon to witness and gives the garden designer the best kind of job satisfaction.

Traditionally, planting schemes involved flowers, shrubs and trees in nice, neat rows, with colour being introduced by the addition of summer bedding plants. It was a very expensive and labour-intensive method. Many people today enjoy tending their own garden, but, because of the demands of a busy lifestyle, they have limited time available for its maintenance. They may aim to spend only a few hours a week keeping their outdoor space neat and tidy, using it primarily for relaxation and recuperation, or entertainment.

Another type of gardening that is becoming increasingly popular is the more practical 'grow your own'. More and more garden owners have been having a go at the small-scale growing of vegetables, salads and fruit, usually starting with the easier stuff, like lettuce, onions and potatoes. Eating your own home-grown produce gives a great sense of achievement and satisfaction, so a kitchen garden area may be on your wish list. When dealing with a sloping site, the creation of a flat area (or maybe more than one) will be required for this purpose. Size wise, it will need to be in keeping with the available space, the gardener's skills and ambitions, and the time they have available for maintenance. ptions range from the grandest layout of several ground-level veg beds, raised beds, a greenhouse, compost area and cold frames to the more manageable, much smaller affair of a couple of raised beds for the hobbyist.

When planning the planting in general, the type and style required will vary enormously from person to person. Some will be looking for a scheme that requires the absolute minimum amount of maintenance and care, while others will want a stylized, high-maintenance design, perhaps in Italianate or cottage garden style. The contemporary cottage garden, for example, involves high numbers of plants, many of which are perennials, which require regular and time-consuming maintenance such as cutting back, splitting and moving, and will all die back in the autumn leaving a bare patch of ground.. Other schemes rely on the prima donnas of the plant world, which demand very specific growing conditions. Sometimes, a client's desired planting style may just not be appropriate for the soil and aspect of a particular site, in which case the designer will need to advise accordingly and look at alternatives.

Table 2.1 Questionnaire to form the brief

HARD LANDSCAPING						
DESIGN STYLE:	Formal/linear	Informal/curves	Contemporary	Garden rooms		
Advice given						
FEATURES:	Patio	Pergola	Decking	Steps	Water feature	
Good or poor condition? To be replaced?						
ASPECT:						
Shady side of the garden? Deep shade areas?						
STRUCTURES:	Shed	Summerhouse	Greenhouse	Arbour	Steps	Walls
Existing in poor condition? To be replaced?						
SOFT LANDSCAPING						
TREES:						
Advice given Existing trees – how many require remedial work?						
Require new? Evergreen/deciduous. Ornamental flower, foliage, or berries?						
SHRUBS:						
Advice given Existing shrubs – how many require remedial work?						
Require new? Type of shrubs – evergreen/deciduous. Flower, foliage, or berries?						
Planting style: Seasonal interest	Architectural	Contemporary	Naturalistic			
FENCES: Advice given Existing – need replacing? New to be installed?						
SOIL: Existing – clay base/free-draining/loam						
Advice given						
DRAINAGE: Towards house/away from house?						
Existing drainage channel around house? New drainage to be installed?						
VIEWS:						
Poor/good views?						

Year-round interest is the most frequent request, but this is difficult to achieve, as it requires an in-depth knowledge of all the plant groups. An understanding of what plant goes where, based on soil conditions and the growing requirements of particular plants, will be developed over the years through research and experience. There is heaps of information to hand, but most gardeners carrying out their own project will want to visit the garden centre, buy the plants, and get them planted in a weekend, not spend weeks researching a planting plan. If year-round interest is a priority for you, it may be worth seeking out and paying for professional advice.

Putting Together the Brief

Once you have done your analysis and written your assessment, you will be ready to progress to creating the brief. The quickest and easiest way to do this is by using a questionnaire (*see* Table 2.1). You can sit down and complete this yourself for your own project or go through it with the client if you are working on someone else's garden.

A garden designer working with a client may need to include further topics in the questionnaire, to identify not only what needs to be done, but also to gain an in-depth understanding of what the client requires, in order to have the garden of their dreams. This may not always be possible. Once the wish list has been established, the acid test in terms of feasibility comes when the conversation turns to money matters. This is the point at which an unrealistic budget will blow everything out the water. To avoid wasting time and energy, it is advisable to establish a rough idea of the budget right at the start of the conversation.

Unfortunately, many clients have very little idea how much they will want or need to spend. Where can the garden designer go from there? The way forward is to continue the conversation, but to make it very clear that, although a wish list may be completed, there are no guarantees that the project will be affordable. In order to gauge the eventual cost of the project, one option at this stage is to develop a scaled plan. This will enable the accurate calculation of slabbed areas and the quantifying of materials for other construction elements such as walls, raised beds and pathways, in order for a contractor to prepare a costing. Because the plan is in sketch format (that is, to scale but all in pencil), any amendments can easily be made to achieve the fulfilment of a budget that suits the client (or yourself, if it is a self-build project).

As you work your way through the tick boxes in order to create a wish list, it becomes clear that the options are many and varied. This may be the point at which reality kicks in, with the realization that Kew Gardens cannot be re-created on a shoestring! The role of the designer is to gently guide the client towards a realistic plan for their particular budget. There are many adjustments that can be made, such as opting for a Riven reconstituted concrete slab as opposed to genuine York stone. Not only is the latter way more expen-

Table 2.2 Client wish list tick boxes

CLIENT REQUIREMENTS/WISH LIST					
Patio		Shed		PLANTING STYLE	
Pergola		Summerhouse		Formal	
Steps		Greenhouse		Informal	
Retaining structures		Kitchen garden area		Low-maintenance	
Other seating areas		Arbour		Cottage	
Barbecue area		Play area		Italianate	
Outdoor kitchen area		Raised beds		Other style	
Layout style – formal		Built-in seating		Lawn	
Informal		Gazebo		Companion planting	
Water feature – pool		Wildlife-friendly		Bee/butterfly friendly	
Water cascade					
Low-maintenance					

Table 2.3 Example of a brief

BRIEF for CLIENT: ....

ADDRESS: .... **WORK REQUIRED:** Re-design rear garden

....

GARDEN PROBLEMS	DESIGN SOLUTIONS
1. Current garden is a small area of slabs outside the patio doors and the rest laid down to lawn.	Re-design with a second seating area in the sun, less lawn, develop the area to rear of garage and make the garden an attractive, functional outdoor space.
2. The garden slopes towards the house.	Split level and create two flat areas.
3. Garden is an open flat space.	Introduce height with both hard landscaping and planting structure.
4. Garden is 'L'-shaped with the arm o f the 'L' behind the garage out of sight.	Develop the area behind the garage with possibly a static water feature or bench seat. Develop a planting scheme for this area which has a striking foliage.
5. Garden has no planting.	Develop a low-maintenance planting scheme that provides seasonal interest with strong winter structure. Client also would like some herbs and a naturalistic, wildlife-friendly planting scheme.
6. Garage wall on the left dominates the garden and is very harsh.	Either move path away from the wall and create a border along to soften the wall or introduce a structure such as a narrow pergola to balance the height and create vertical planting areas.
7. Existing paths in poor condiiton.	Remove, install alternative as per plan.
8. Existing greenhouse and shed are rotten.	Remove – not to be replaced.

To summarize:

This is a new-build house with grass and functional slabbing. It has the potential to be a lovely outdoor space for relaxing and entertaining in different areas. The slope needs split levelling, to create a change of levels which will increase the visual appeal and make the garden more interesting to move around. This blank canvas has lots of potential.

sive, it also tends to involve higher delivery costs to get it to site, as it is not stocked by most garden material outlets.

Roughly speaking, the questions that lead to the creation of a brief deal with the 'hard' elements that make the garden functional, such as patios, steps and retainers, and the more aesthetic 'soft' features that improve the look and enjoyment of the garden. Here again, there are several options – a water feature could be as simple as a wildlife pool or low-maintenance trickling rock at minimal cost. At the other end of the scale, the plan could include an expensive, complicated koi carp pool or water cascade.

There is some overlap between the brief questionnaire and the wish list tick boxes, but a two-pronged approach is useful in order to come up with the answers to the following questions:

- What would be *desirable* if there were few budget limitations? What does the client's (or your) dream garden look like?
- What needs to be done, to make the slope usable?
- What is realistic and feasible within the given budget?

Once the questionnaire has been completed, it can be referred to in the drafting of a text document using the same headings. This document then becomes the brief. It can be shown to the client for their approval and gives them the opportunity to add or remove anything they wish. The brief is also a way of confirming the plan of action, so that every party involved in the project has the same understanding of its aims, timescale and budget.

Developing the Garden Plan

Using the headings of 'hard landscaping' and 'soft landscaping' in the questionnaire is a logical approach to organizing your notes and recording the information. It is then easy to return to either section and check back when you come to developing the garden plan.

The term 'garden plan' may sound very grand, but in the case of a smaller garden with a shallow slope it may not need to be a fully scaled drawing. It could be as simple and quick as a sketch in 'duck egg' format (*see* Fig. 2.7), as a way to start to formulate the desired layout for the garden. The sketch or drawing will enable consideration of where specific areas are to be, and how they will be inter-related and work together. It will also focus minds on the functional, practical aspects of the proposed garden. For instance, it would not be practical to position a barbecue area at the far end of the garden, requiring a long walk from the kitchen. Instead, it should be located on the patio, or as near as possible to the kitchen. A deck should not be located in the shade for safety reasons.

The 'duck egg' method requires no technical drawing skills, scaled rulers or use of CAD (computer-aided-design), so it can easily be used by anybody. If necessary, the sketch can then be used as a guide for the development of a fully scaled plan if the size and complexity of the sloping garden demands this.

At this stage, the plan is a more relaxed exploration of 'what goes where', and highlights how the areas relate to each other when they are being used. As the 'duck eggs' are quick and easy to draw, it is possible to explore several layouts in the minimum amount of time. The exact position of steps and retainers will be

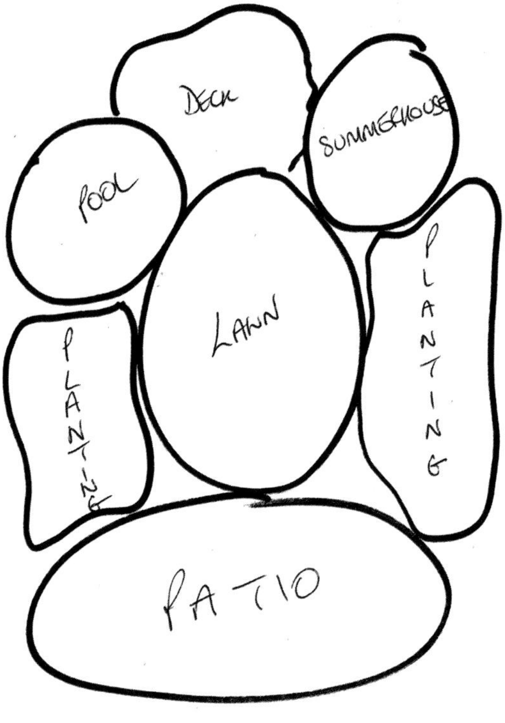

Fig. 2.7 'Duck egg' sketch.

added later when you start to look in more detail at the slope and its relation to access points from the house. It is a given that, if there are bi-fold, patio or French doors, they should open on to a hard surface such as a patio or path. Whether using the 'duck egg' method or drafting a scaled plan, you will be able to return to the brief and use it as a double check to systematically work through the list.

The importance of gathering as much information as possible prior to beginning the plan for any garden project cannot be emphasized enough. When working for a client, a detailed brief will act as an insurance that everything the client requires will end up in the plan, and should prevent any confusion or disagreements later on in the project. When working on your own project, the brief will be a very useful 'aide memoire', to ensure that the end result is everything you want it to be. Whether the garden is sloping or flat, the same preparation and structured approach is advisable for any garden project, regardless of its size.

CHAPTER 3

SURVEYING AND USING SECTION DRAWINGS

Engaging with the Site

After the questionnaire, wish lists, briefs and plans have been discussed and explored, it is time to move on to the survey. As you start to work physically with the garden, you will be building a strong knowledge base that will act as a firm foundation to underpin any future work, and ensure that the project is completed to a satisfactory level. A detailed survey of the slope (or slopes) is a top priority when working with a sloping site. It will provide you with an understanding that will enable you to satisfy the demands of a client, an owner and those involved in the construction, and achieve the right level of both safety and functionality.

During the survey, time spent working carefully not just on the site but also *with* the site will result in a productive working relationship and knowledge base. Even an average survey of a relatively flat garden, with straight boundaries, a simple lawn, a number of borders, and no barriers to measuring, such as large trees, shrubs and garden structures, involves a lot of walking around and can take several hours. The positioning of base tapes, taking measurements along those tapes, deciding on the location of triangulation points and scrambling through bushes to get to the fence line are all parts of a time-consuming yet enjoyable exercise. The sloping garden takes even more time and effort in order to gain a real understanding of its nuances. Due consideration of the slope direction, whether straight down, to the left or right, or all three, along with diligent measuring to represent the slope graphically in the form of sections, can seem rather long-winded, but it is time well spent.

The order of the day will be making multiple journeys walking up and down the slope to take change of level (COL) measurements. When calculated, these will enable you to draw sections of the slope as it is. It is advisable to take several of these COL measurement lines, to give a visual representation of the slope across the entire garden. Take central, left and right measurement lines from the top to the bottom of the slope, so that when you are looking at designing in steps, retainers or flat areas in more than one area, such as towards the sides or across the garden, the information required to calculate these will be to hand. If you are working for a client, it is better to spend longer on one visit than to have to return another day because you have not taken enough measurements.

The survey process provides a unique personal *physical* experience of the site: at a basic level you will be able to judge how steep or shallow the slope is (known as the gradient) by noticing how breathless you are or how much your leg muscles ache! This physical experience of using the site will in turn set off a train of thought that will help you to pinpoint the key issues, and work out what needs to be done in order to improve the site and the ease with which people will be able to move around it. It is much less taxing to traverse, or walk across, a slope than trying to walk straight up or down it. This is why in some well-known public gardens, such as Powis Castle in Wales, there are pathways that run across the slope, making it easier and more comfortable for visitors of varying physical abilities to get around the garden. This technique can also allow enough space for the creation of large, long planting beds which are level and therefore easier to maintain.

During the survey 'walk around', you may notice a wonderful view from the far end of the garden, which is perhaps almost central. As you stop to take it in, you might be inspired to think about a central flight of steps with a flat sitting area halfway down, from which the panorama can be enjoyed again and again. On the other hand, you may become aware that, from about halfway down, the slope is shallower, maybe almost flat, and that it overlooks an unattractive building. When you have identified a view like this, which is less than desirable, you will want to consider how it may be screened – maybe a planted area with some ornamental trees, instead of hard landscaping, or a pergola with vertical planting. There are many options.

As you engage with the sloping site and experience it for yourself, ideas will begin to flow in direct response to the experience. These should be noted or sketched alongside the survey notes, with photographs taken as an additional aid to your memory. This reference material can be returned to repeatedly, and eventually may become part of the final design proposals.

Practicalities of Carrying Out a Survey

A site survey has a number of purposes:

- It is an overview/examination, to ascertain the condition and quality of the site.

Fig. 3.1 Slope at Powis Castle, near Welshpool, with a path running across the slope.

- It is an opportunity to map or plan the site.
- A chance to account for the particulars of the site – in other words, the slope.
- It is an opportunity to take analysis notes.

The RHS (Royal Horticultural Society) examiners give a clear definition of garden survey. Briefly, it states that it is 'the detailed surveying/measuring and recording of a garden together with features and services' (30 December 2020). This is a short and to the point summary, but in practice there is much more to be done! To expand upon the basic definition, and give more practical detail, take a copy of the following list when you carry out the survey, so that you miss nothing out.

Remember that you should be taking and recording measurements on the site in order to establish or identify the following:

- The site boundaries.
- The position of buildings (the house, garage, and so on).
- The position of downspouts, drains and manhole covers.
- The position and size of structures (shed, summerhouse, arbour, greenhouse, pergola, and so on).
- Areas for re-location of structures or placement of new structures.
- Areas for specific garden purposes (kitchen garden area, patio, and so on).
- The position of fixed objects such as pools.
- Fixed areas such as drives and pathways if they are to remain.
- The position and shape of beds and borders. Are they to remain, be reshaped or be removed?
- The position of trees and shrubs that are to be removed or require remedial work. (Note that this will incur costs for both labour and disposal.)
- Places where good views may be enjoyed.
- Places where poor views may need to be screened.
- Areas of sun and shade.
- Places where the garden is overlooked.

As well as making note of all these features and possibilities, take photographs all over the site.

Clearly, an accurate survey, with its volume of specific information about the garden, is vital to the successful design and planning of any site, and especially important when dealing with the complexities of a sloping garden. There is a purpose to all this measuring, calculating and plotting. The survey is the first stage in a process that ultimately results in the production of a scaled existing site plan, with analysis notes. This plan will act as a foundation from which everything else will be planned and calculated.

Table 3.1 shows the sequence of events that follows on from the survey, most of which will have an impact on the budget. When working with a client, the scaled plans are integral to the ultimate success or failure of

Table 3.1 The survey to plan process

Taking survey measurements	=	A scale plan of the existing garden
A scale plan of the existing garden	=	Scaled design plans
Accurate meaurements and calculations of materials required	=	Accurate costing of materials
Accurate calculation of materials required and labour for construction	=	Accurate costing of labour
Scaled design/layout plan	=	Used as a template for the planting plan
Scaled planting plan	=	Accurate calculation of plant numbers
Accurate calculation of plant numbers	=	Accurate calculation/costing of labour for planting
Scaled planting plan	=	Accurate calculation and costing of membrane, tree bark and turf if required

the project, but it is equally important to plan ahead when working on your own garden project. Having to leave a project unfinished due to budget issues is most frustrating, unless from the onset the plan has been to work in predetermined 'stages'. Such a decision will probably be based on your early costings.

It is tempting to assume that a smaller site does not need the same level of involvement as a larger one. However, caution should prevail. A small site still demands the same amount of information, as well as a scaled plan to accurately calculate material quantities and labour, thus avoiding any budget issues.

Survey Equipment

The accuracy and efficiency of any survey relies on using the right equipment and tools for the job. That is not to say that large amounts of money need to be spent on the purchase of expensive kit to carry out a more than satisfactory survey in any average-sized garden. One exception would be a large site with a steep slope, but rather than spend money on kit you may not ever use again, in that case it may be preferable to engage the services of a professional land survey company. This not only avoids a significant outlay but also ensures the highest level of accuracy. Equipment available for land surveying ranges from the more expensive and complicated to use items, to the easy-to-use standard long-length tapes. One thing that should be avoided at all costs is a short tape, which you will have to keep moving!

The following items of equipment are the most commonly used:

- Theodolite and staff: quite complicated to use, mostly used for large gardens and steep slopes. Can be expensive to purchase, but may be hired.
- Tapes: easy-to-use long tapes are available from 20m up to 100m long, and are comparatively cheap.
- Measuring wheels: good for measuring large distances. Not fully accurate on uneven ground.
- Spirit level and rotary laser level: can be used for taking linear and levels measurements.
- Hand-held laser measure: not always wholly accurate when shrubs, tree trunks and structures obstruct the beam. Moderate cost.
- Total station: like a theodolite but does a lot more. Normally used for large construction engineering-type projects. Expensive.

Survey Methods

Theodolite and Staff

The theodolite is a very accurate instrument used in surveying mainly for the following purposes:

- Measuring horizontal and vertical angles.
- Locating points on a line.
- Finding the difference in elevations/heights.

Instructions for setting up a theodolite will be provided with the instrument for onsite reference. The method requires two people, one looking through the instrument and recording measurements and the other holding the staff.

The theodolite must be positioned on a flat, level surface, known as the 'base station', and must be measured in at a known point. It is always advisable to use the house as a baseline, as it is a fixed line and is usually square on to the garden.

The person holding the staff moves along a tape that runs down the slope, and records their position as a

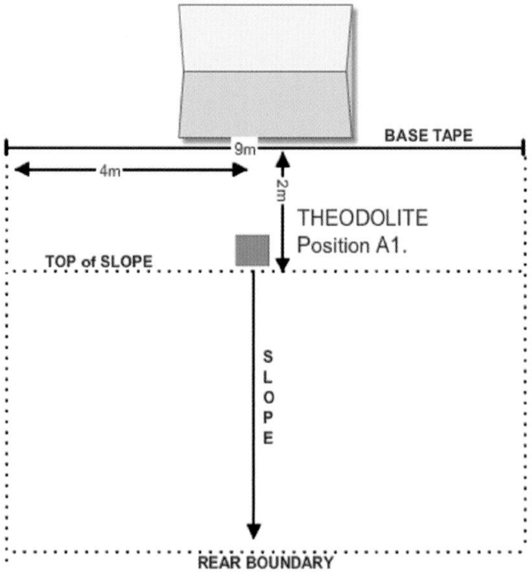

Fig. 3.2 Setting up and positioning of a theodolite.

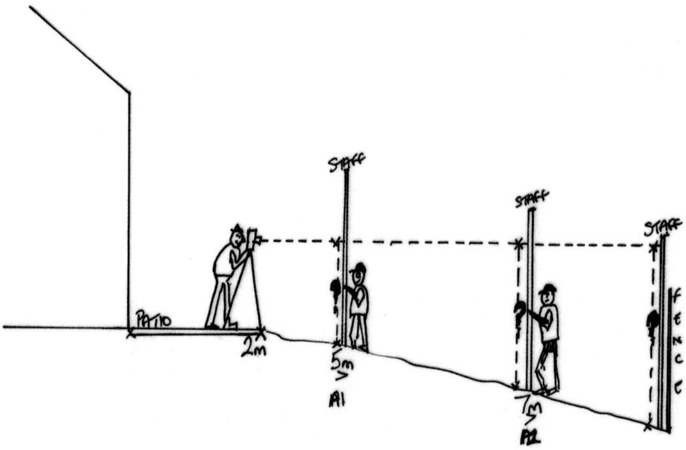

Fig. 3.3 Taking measurements at known points down a slope.

measurement along the tape – this is a known point. At each known point, a reading on the staff is taken looking through the theodolite, and recorded as A1, A2, and so on.

Tapes Method

For a flat garden, the process is as for the theodolite and staff method, with the addition of taking triangulation measurements to pinpoint the position of structures, trees, and any other permanent objects.

Spirit-Level Method for Taking COL Measurements

1. Find a straight piece of wood, preferably of an exact length, such as 2 metres or more. Using a 2-metre length spirit level makes it even easier!
2. Start at the top of the slope and choose a level, permanent feature such as a manhole cover, low wall or step.
3. Measure out from this point. Use the piece of wood or the spirit level and drive in a peg to the height of the permanent feature.
4. Place the piece of wood or spirit level on top of this peg. If you are using a plain piece of wood, check its level using a standard spirit level.
5. Using a hand tape, measure the vertical distance from the piece of wood or spirit level to the ground.
6. Bang in a peg to mark the spot.
7. Move the piece of wood or spirit level to this spot and take the vertical measurement again.
8. Repeat this process until you reach the bottom of the slope.
9. Add up each of the vertical measurements (*see* Fig. 3.4): 0.300 + 0.500 + 0.200 = 1000mm/100cm or 1 metre. The total will give the overall change of level.

Rotary Laser Level

A rotary laser level can be used for taking linear and levels measurements. The method requires two people, as with the theodolite and staff.

Taking Measurements

Taking survey measurements involves several techniques, all of which have a specific purpose. In most

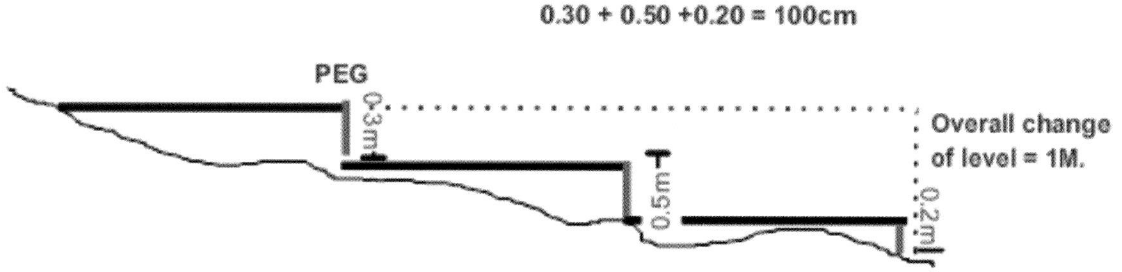

Fig. 3.4 The spirit-level method.

gardens there are a huge variety of irregular shapes to be found, in the form of borders and lawns, and the overall shape of the site itself. Somehow these need to be measured accurately, using a variety of techniques.

There are a number of different types of measurement, with specific purposes:

- Linear measurements: basic survey measurements, usually straight or as straight as possible.
- Triangulation: for plotting the position of boundary corners to determine the exact shape of the plot; also for plotting the position of structures, trees, manhole covers and other objects.
- Running measurements: taken along base tape to plot windows, doors, drains, and so on; can also be used to plot large plants in a border.
- Offsets: used to plot a curved edge and or to record large plants in a border.

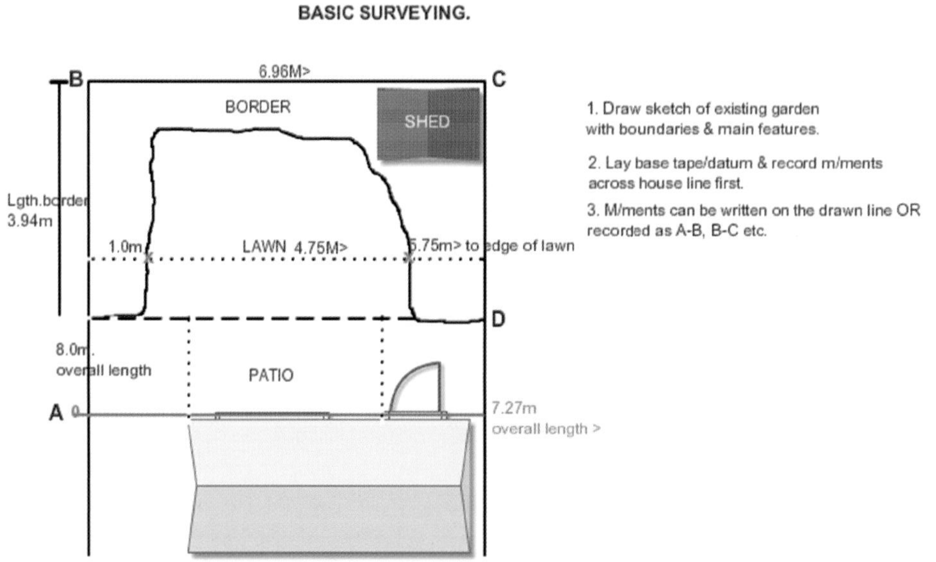

Fig. 3.5 Basic surveying.

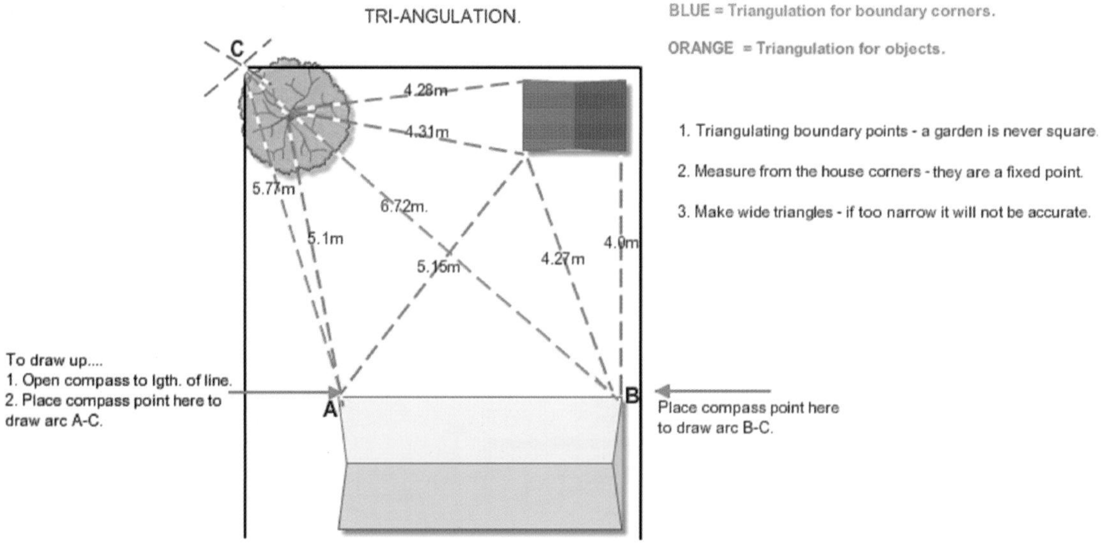

Fig. 3.6 Triangulation.

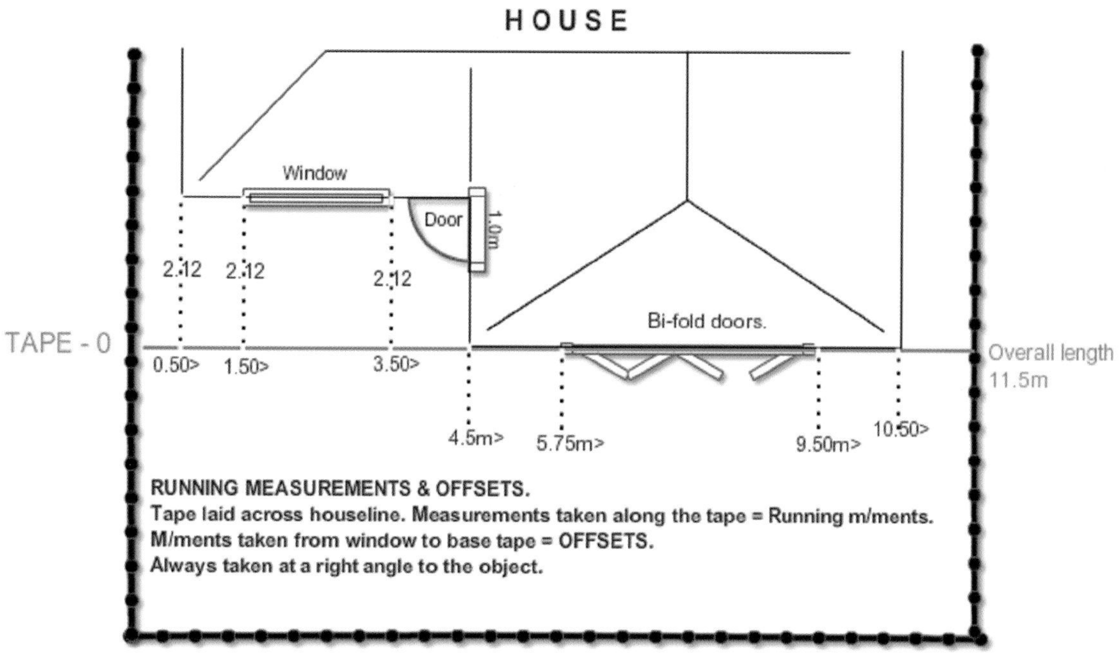

Fig. 3.7 Running measurements and offsets.

How to Do a Basic Survey

1. Get yourself a notepad or a sheet of paper – A3 is a useful size – along with something to lean on, such as a clipboard, several long-length tape measures and a hand tape, or whatever survey equipment you are using.
2. Draw a basic outline of the garden (*see* Fig. 3.5).
3. Set the base tape across the house line and start with taking running measurements along this tape across the house line, recording them on your sketch. It is important to mark the direction in which the measurements are taken with a small arrow, and to label doors, windows, drains, patio, and so on.
4. Once you have completed the house line measurements, begin taking boundary measurements, including triangulation of the garden corners, structures, manhole covers and trees.
5. Follow with measuring in borders, beds, ponds, gates, and access points.
6. Take an 'N' point (most smartphones have a compass on them).
7. Take photos of all the elements, including manhole covers, examples of poor construction or condition (crumbling walls, steps, fencing and structures), as well as weak, diseased or overgrown trees and shrubs.
8. Take measurements around the garden using the various techniques (*see* Figs 3.3, 3.6 and 3.7).
9. Take levels measurements using an appropriate method: theodolite and staff for taking measurements at known points (*see* Fig. 3.3), or spirit level (*see* Fig. 3.4).

Drawing to Scale and Sections

Once back at the office desk or kitchen table, you will be ready to move on to the next stage, which involves converting the survey measurements into an existing site plan drawn to scale.

When a drawing is described as being 'drawn to scale', it means that each element in that drawing is in the same proportion in relation to the real or proposed thing. Scale rulers can be purchased with a variety of

Table 3.2 Drawing scales

1:1	Same size as the original	
1:10	10 times smaller	1M = 4in
1:20	20 times smaller – useful for construction drawings	1M = 2in
1:50	Most commonly used scale for garden design plans – a whole garden will fit on an A1 piece of paper	1M = 1in
1:100	Used for large gardens – a whole garden will fit on an A1 piece of paper	1M = 1cm or ½in.
1:200	Used for extremely large sites – probably several acres	1M = ½cm or ¼in

scales on them and are inexpensive at a few pounds each. For the purposes of drawing garden design plans to scale, a ruler with 1:20, 1:50 and 1:100 will suffice.

Drawing the site to scale to draft an existing site plan is where all your copious notes and measurements start to take shape, to become something you can see and measure from. For a sloping site, a levels survey will have been done, using one of the usual methods. In addition to preparing an existing site plan, you will also need to plot the levels measurement lines – A–B, A–C, and so on – on the plan in the position from which the measurements were taken (*see* Fig. 3.8). The gradient of the slope may also be calculated from the levels measurements taken (*see* Fig. 3.9). A total overall change of level is arrived at, giving the change of level from the top (the highest point of the slope) to the bottom (the lowest point of the slope).

Once you have the calculations, they can be used to produce a visual representation of the slope, known as a section. A 'section drawing', 'section' or 'sectional drawing' as used in garden design shows a view of a slope as though it had been sliced in half. Sections, in

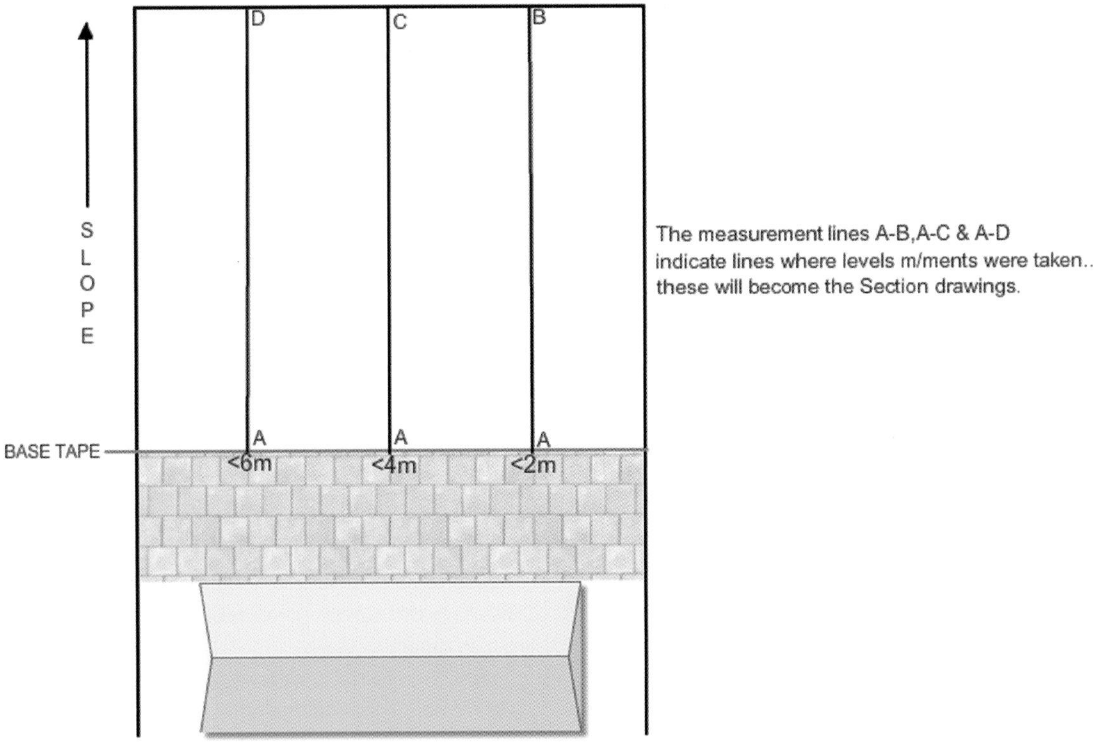

Fig. 3.8 Plotting levels measurement lines.

Fig. 3.9 Taking and calculating levels measurements.

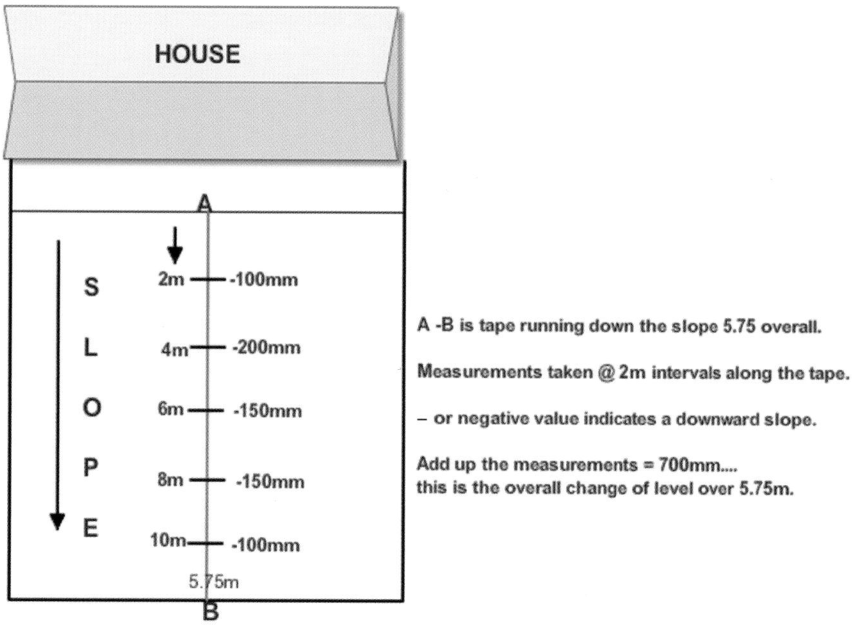

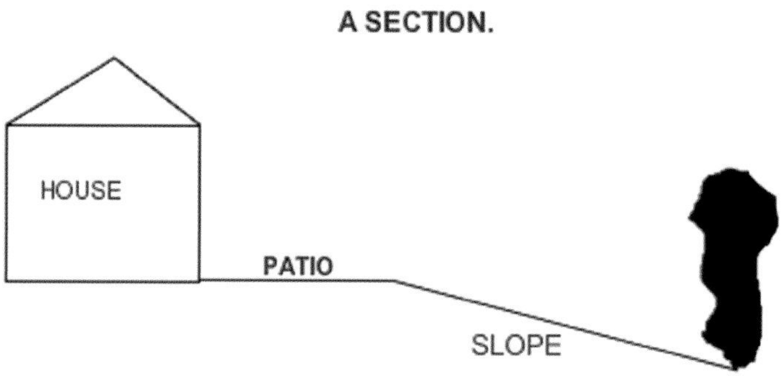

Fig. 3.10 Section drawing.

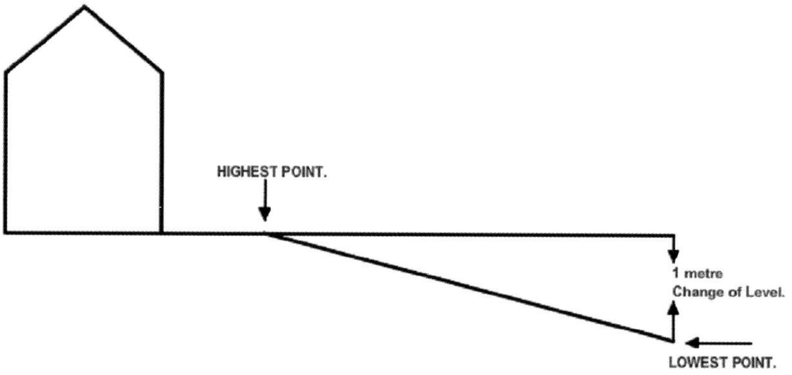

Fig. 3.11 Section drawing of overall change of level.

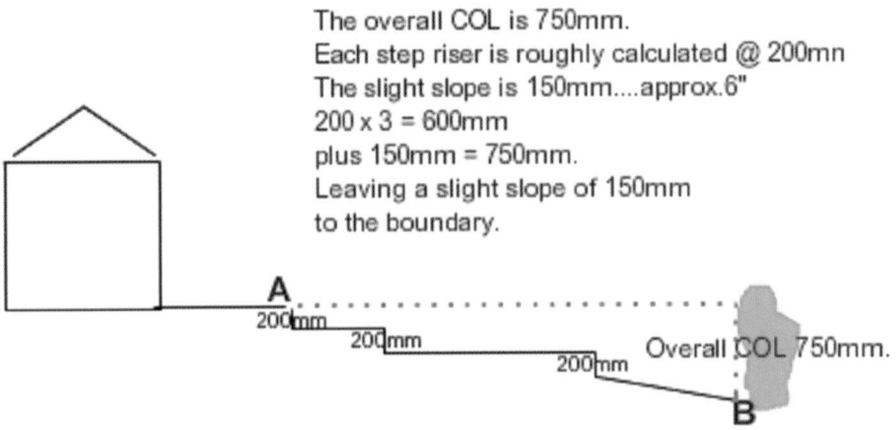

Fig. 3.12 Section drawing of proposed levels A–B.

their simplest form, are used to calculate and show the position of steps and flat areas, and the height of retaining structures. More layers can be added such as planting but first and foremost, the drawing is a calculation tool.

Calculating for Steps

A section drawing of the existing slope allows you to visualize the slope and clearly see the gradient that you are working with. When considering the construction of a flight of steps, section drawings are drawn to scale so that the number of steps can be calculated accurately. This is done by using a simple calculation of dividing the overall change of level by 200 – 200mm is the recommended maximum riser height. Of course, there may be a variation in the riser height – 150mm is the recommended minimum. Dividing the overall change of level by 200 is a quick, easy calculation at this stage for the purpose of working to scale and in order to find the number of steps required. The riser height will be affected by the materials used to construct it. Where a contractor is involved, it is usually their role to make the final, more precise calculations. There is more detail on this in Chapter 4.

Gradients

Although the term 'gradient' is more usually associated with landscape architecture, it is useful for the garden designer to have an understanding of its meaning. It refers to the use of figures to describe the 'steepness' or 'shallowness' of a slope. It may be expressed in two ways, either as a ratio or a percentage. A warning sign at the top or bottom of a steep road, for example, will show drivers the gradient as a percentage.

The rise/run of a slope is the distance travelled *vertically* divided by the distance travelled *horizontally*. To express that figure as a percentage, it is multiplied by 100. So, for example, if you go up 5 feet as you go forwards 100 feet, the slope has a gradient of 5 per cent.

A slope may also be expressed as a ratio – for example, 4:1, which indicates that for every 4 units (feet or metres) of horizontal distance, there is a 1 unit (foot or metre) vertical change either up or down.

Fig. 3.14 Hill sign showing its gradient as a percentage.

Cut and Fill

For every step or set of steps there will normally be an area of flat ground, to allow movement from one place to another. The garden may have other level areas, for seating and to accommodate other garden structures such as a shed, summerhouse or greenhouse. Usually, there will be a level hard surface area outside the rear door, and most gardeners also like to have one or more level lawn areas. A steep sloping lawn is difficult to mow and maintain, and cannot be used for impromptu games of football, cricket or tennis.

In the world of garden and landscape design, flat areas are created by using a technique commonly known as 'cut and fill', which involves moving soil from one area to another. When used on a sloping site, it is known as 'regrading' the slope. All the excavated soil is kept within the site and redistributed, so the cut and fill method represents a considerable reduction in environmental impact. On a large site, there is potentially a significant amount of soil or 'spoil'. Removing this from site and transporting it to a specialist soil dump is an expensive exercise, so cut and fill also reduces costs. Both the environmental and budget benefits mean that the method is very much in favour these days.

The section drawing can clearly show where the level area needs to be. A line drawn outwards shows where the 'cut' should be taken from and where the soil is to be redistributed to the 'fill' area, creating a flat space. When it is drawn to scale as a section, the contractor can measure to scale and not only accurately calculate the quantities of soil to be moved around, but also determine whether any additional soil needs to be brought in for areas to be made up.

Currently, it is common practice and positively encouraged for soil to be moved around and redistributed on site where the steepness gradient of a slope needs to be reduced. It is a design option that will produce a beautiful, naturalistic, undulating effect to the landform. If the slope is shallow, it is possible to eradicate it completely by redistributing soil around the site to 'regrade' it (*see* Chapter 4).

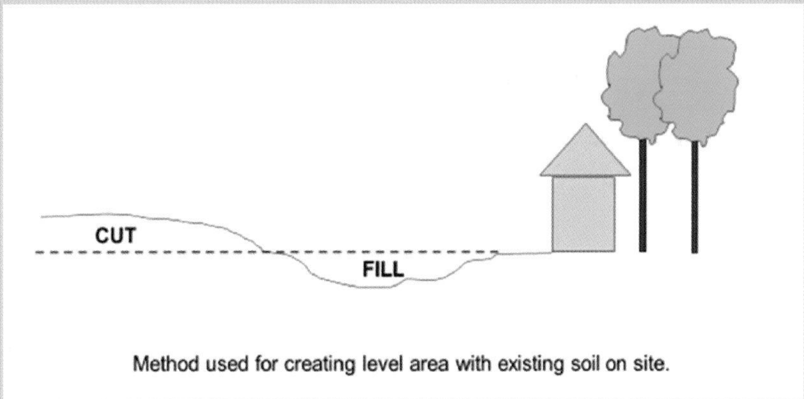

Fig. 3.13 Cut and fill.

It is not often that a garden designer would be required to calculate a gradient, but it may be necessary when considering access for a wheelchair user or someone with limited mobility. In this case, you might decide to include a ramp. The construction of an element such as this would need to adhere to current regulations and guidelines, so you would be well advised to carry out some research. There are some basic guidelines in Chapter 4.

The Overlay Method

The overlay method has been around for many years and there are several uses for it in garden design and planning. It is such a simple technique but so useful. When working on the more technical aspects of a project, such as calculating existing and proposed levels, the method is used for preparing section drawings, and it can also be used for the preparation of more artistic sketches used to present ideas to clients (*see* Chapter 4).

The overlay method (*see* Fig. 3.15) is a more specific version for working to scale to produce section drawings. It is a graphics technique which can be used both to critically assess existing levels and to inform and design new proposed levels. (For its other uses, *see* Chapter 4).

The overlay method is as follows:

1. Draw a section of the existing slope, to scale, on paper.
2. Lay a piece of tracing paper over the top and fix it in place.
3. Working from point A on the house line, use a scale ruler to draw in flat areas – such as paving or lawn – to the desired size and link these with steps. Use 200mm for risers and 300–450mm deep for treads (the flat part of a step that your foot lands on; *see* Fig. 3.16). Continue working along this line to point B on the boundary.
4. If more than one levels measurement line has been taken, additional sections can be drawn labelled as

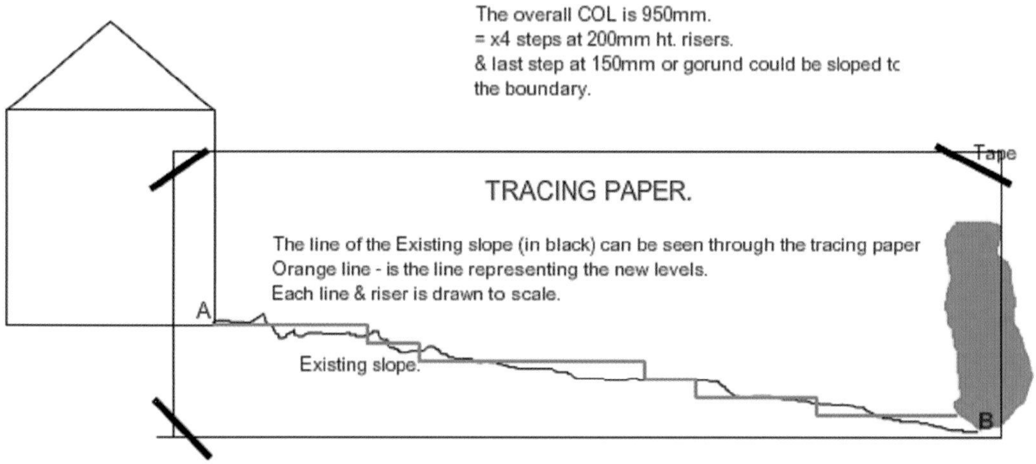

Fig. 3.15 The overlay method.

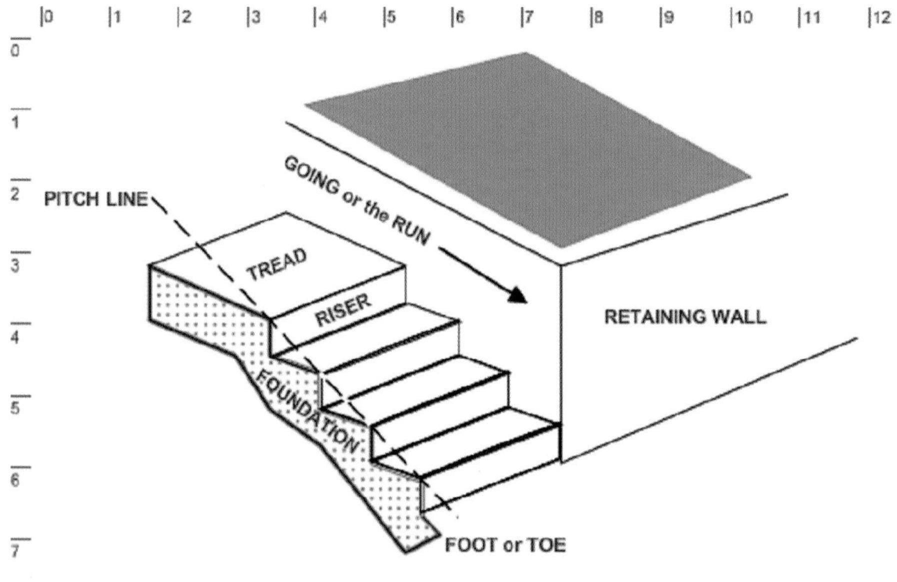

Fig. 3.16 The anatomy of a step.

per the line indicated on the existing site plan: A–B, A–C, A–D, and so on. This allows for cross reference between the existing site plan and the section drawings.

5. When drawing the sections, consider the flat areas as either hard landscaping or lawn to help estimate their size.

When you think the survey is finished, take a few moments to check that you have covered those small details that are so easily forgotten: whether doors open in or out, the width of access points, where the N point is. Make sure they are all recorded on the sketch – you do not want to have to make a special journey back to site for one small detail, especially if its several miles away.

Measuring-up techniques are the same for any site, regardless of size. It is a very logical procedure and one that gets quicker the more surveys you do. The key is to take your time, work at your own pace and fully focus on the job in hand. Take copious photographs or video, with lots of close-up shots and recorded informative comments. Visual reminders are invaluable. Certain aspects of the garden may seem very clear to you at the time, but can be easily forgotten a few weeks down the line.

CHAPTER 4

DESIGN CONSIDERATIONS

Safe and easy access on a sloping site is provided by steps, landings and ramps, mostly one or the other but sometimes a combination of all three. If the garden is to be used by someone who has limited mobility, a wheelchair user or perhaps an older person who relies on a walking stick or frame, it will be necessary to incorporate flat areas and ramps. Without these elements, a sloping site can pose a very difficult and potentially dangerous challenge. Fortunately, there is increasing awareness of the need to provide safe and easy access in all locations.

Fig. 4.1 An exotic sloping garden.

Often, where steps are installed, there will be a retaining structure on either side of them. Similarly, when a large slope is being split-levelled or terraced, vertical retaining structures will be needed to hold back the earth where each flat terrace is to be created. With this in mind, this chapter is divided into three sections, covering steps, retaining structures and ramps.

Steps

The practicalities of step design are usually what come to mind as soon as you start to consider introducing steps into a garden – they are, after all, primarily

Fig. 4.2 Basic steps.

a means to negotiate a slope and/or changes of level safely and quickly. However, they may also be seen as presenting a window of opportunity, if the designer chooses to make a feature of them.

Steps as a Design Feature

The job of a designer when planning steps is not only to ensure safety but also to bring a broader vision into the mix, to create something interesting, attractive and exciting in the garden. Try to 'think outside the box' and consider a wider role for them, which is not just about the functionality of the step as a step. Plan ahead and consider all the options, to avoid any long-term regrets over not having done something more interesting.

So, when is a step not a step? There are several answers to this question: when it is a retaining structure; when it is a seat; when it is a focal point feature. The designer will envision the step as something that can bring more to a garden than a simple means of getting from A to B. The degree to which this opportunity can be exploited may be limited when working within a restricted budget, in which case the designer will propose a more basic, purely practical set of steps (*see* Fig. 4.2). Steps can be made more aesthetically pleasing by paying attention to the choice of materials and the way in which those materials are used. For example, bricks may be laid in a variety of patterns – a stronger pattern will certainly catch the eye more than a simple one, creating a focal point feature.

A basic set of steps, such as those in Fig. 4.2, may have a low visual impact, with nothing very striking or attractive about them. It can be a useful exercise to look at and critically analyse such low-impact hard land-

Fig. 4.3 Bricks in a straight pattern.

Fig. 4.4 Bricks laid in a herring-bone pattern.

scaping elements – steps, walls, and so on – and come up with ideas about how they could be improved. Take photographs and study them in detail, making notes as to what you think might be lacking, and develop those observations into concepts of what could be altered to make them more of a feature. An analysis of the steps in Fig. 4.2 might read something like this:

- The overall shape is very 'boxy'.
- The muted colour of materials used is very bland.
- There is no individual element that appeals to the eye.
- They leave no impression upon the viewer.
- They are purely functional, allowing safe access from the lower to upper level.

If simple functionality is what is required, or if the budget is relatively low, a basic set-up is of course perfectly acceptable, but it is so much more interesting to attempt to make a feature of steps. While the question of what is aesthetically pleasing is always subjective, any gardener will appreciate steps that function in more than one way. They may provide seating, become part of a water feature, or perform the role of a split-level retaining structure. If a more generous budget is available, there will be more options available and the design proposal can be more adventurous and less predictable, resulting in a striking feature to be enjoyed for many years to come.

Shape, Materials and Colour

Clearly, a project with a generous budget presents the designer or owner with the opportunity to take a more creative approach to steps and make a bold statement in the garden. There may well be challenges of a practical nature, in terms of making the most efficient use of often limited space and trying to manage the building of a feature that demands the use of skilled labour. However, it is possible to create steps that will be a talking point, more than simply functional and good to look at. In order to achieve this, broadly speaking there are three aspects of step design to be considered in more depth:

- the shape;
- the materials and how they are used; and
- the colour.

The steps in Fig. 4.5 were designed using dynamic curves, which make them so much more interesting and exciting to look at. As it changes, the curved line makes the eye want to follow it, making a relatively small space look bigger. Of course, these steps featured in a show garden, but that does not mean that they are not relevant to every gardener or garden designer. The very purpose of a show garden is to attract attention, stimulate creative thought and motivate the observer to

Fig. 4.5 Striking steps.

reproduce or adapt the ideas in their own space. Even in a small garden, the essence of the concept can be repeated, albeit on a reduced scale. This particular set of steps has been designed to be a feature, to provide a talking point that is also a means of access to the upper level. A critical analysis on these steps might read something like this:

- Shape – use of dynamic curves – makes the eye follow the line – Flow.
- Colour – white and bright – attracts the eye; reflects, and increases, light.
- Interesting edge – low, evergreen planting strips create low-level planting interest – not only soften the step edge but also cleverly define and highlight the edge to prevent a trip hazard.

Scale/Size

Scale is 'the size of an object in relation to another object and to its surroundings generally'. For example, if a particularly tall building has a two-foot-high hedge planted around it, the two elements will appear 'out of scale' with each other. The balance of the design will be wrong, with the hedge being completely dominated by the building.

The same guidelines apply when considering steps and terraces. A wide terrace will benefit from wide steps, preferably the same width as the terrace, or as near as possible. A wide terrace with narrow steps can look distinctly odd as the two elements will be out of scale with each other. Similarly, terracing can look distinctly odd when several terraces are broken up with a number of flights of small, narrow steps. Chopping up the space into smaller, blocky areas will make it seem disjointed and less generous. More width will emphasize horizontal surfaces and give the garden a greater sense of space by encouraging the eye to move outwards. Correspondingly, if a pathway is 1.5m wide, the steps should be designed to be the same width rather than creating a restriction to easy movement with narrower steps.

If they are big enough, steps can also act as a series of split-level retaining structures, which could have been a wall with one flight of much smaller steps. Finally, when considering scale in step design, if the flight of steps is a long one then it is advisable to provide a landing every four to six steps. This allows the user to take a break on their way up or down, which is particularly important if they are to be used by older people and those with limited mobility.

Multi-Purpose Steps

Terracing

Terracing involves a slope being divided into several levels, each created with a retaining structure and steps for access to each. Each flat area can incorporate beds for planting, to soften and enhance the structural elements.

Steps as a Water Feature

Working on a sloping garden presents the gardener or designer with an ideal set of circumstances in which to create a particularly impressive type of water feature – a water cascade. A slope provides the ideal ground form

Fig. 4.6 Terracing.

Fig. 4.7 Steps as a feature that also provides seating.

Step Design at its Most Inspiring

There are many examples of step design, past and present, which can be simple, incredibly detailed and often complex. Steps can be so much more than just steps – *see* Figs 4.8 to 4.13. Some examples may be really 'grandiose', and would be completely out of place in the average garden, but they can act as inspiration in terms of shape, use of materials and other ideas to install feature steps. One common thread links all the sites: each had a considerable slope that demanded significant development to allow the garden owners and their visitors to go up or down it, and to enable access to the rest of the garden. Each designer has taken full advantage of the opportunity to create a 'wow' factor in each case.

ABOVE LEFT: Fig. 4.8 Beautiful stone steps.

ABOVE RIGHT: Fig. 4.9 Steps designed by the prolific and highly respected American landscape architect Fletcher Steele (1885–1971).

LEFT: FIG. 4.10 Water steps at Chatsworth House in Derbyshire.

Fig. 4.11 Sheffield Peace Gardens.

Fig. 4.12 The Eden Project in Cornwall.

Fig. 4.13 Steps at Kiftsgate Court Gardens in Gloucestershire.

Fig. 4.14 Steps as a water feature Hestercombe Gardens, near Taunton in Somerset.

Fig. 4.15 Steps with a water feature designed in.

for a cascade that looks natural and as if it has been there for years, and this can be incorporated with a set of steps. The key for this to work effectively is a sufficiently powerful pump through which the water is pumped back to the top of the slope. For more practical advice and information on the materials required for such a feature, have a look at the website of watersidenursery.co.uk.

Design Criteria

Clearly, a step is not just a step! The initial design approach can make a huge difference to the final overall impression and functionality of steps and terraces. The end result will depend upon the criteria of whether the slope simply needs steps for access, or whether it is a garden problem that can be resolved by creating a feature of the steps.

The success or otherwise of the feature will depend upon the initial choices

Fig. 4.16 A small cascade created with steps.

made between the client or owner and designer. The end goal is to achieve steps that are functional, that enable easy and safe access to the slope and that are aesthetically pleasing.

Early design decisions can be made based on a number of questions:

- Are steps required at all? Can the slope be regraded? This is a decision with two influential factors: budget and whether a naturalistic style is required, which would be achieved with regrading.
- Is the slope difficult to navigate without steps or a ramp?
- Will installing steps improve the aesthetics of the slope and garden?
- Will installing steps enable the development and maintenance of areas of the garden that are currently inaccessible because of the slope? The client or owner may wish to develop these areas.
- Does the slope run towards the house? If so, it may be necessary to install drainage. In this case, terracing is the option that will provide more functional flat areas. It is advisable to include drainage at the base of each retaining structure to prevent puddling/pooling outside the house, which will probably be a flat patio area.
- Does the slope run away from the house? If it does, consideration needs to be given to the height of planting and any structures that the owner may want to see from the house.

In most gardens, there are a number of reasons why steps may be used:

- To prevent erosion by wear and tear on soil, turf and planted areas.
- To force a break in the way that users move around the garden, to guide them to a location with a great view or to highlight a hazard.
- To allow easy movement up and down slopes while keeping the feet flat (to avoid overstretching the calf muscles).
- To emphasize an entrance to a building.
- To emphasize and enable access to other garden areas.
- To create interest and pattern.
- To create a retainer (in the case of large steps), which will be more attractive than a flat wall and distribute the weight of retained soil over a bigger area.
- To move from one level to another (although a ramp may be easier, especially if the maintenance of the garden involves regular moving of heavy or cumbersome equipment, such as a mower).
- To connect and link areas of the garden or terrace.
- To control the pace through the garden. For example, narrow, shallow or steep steps tend to impart a sense of urgency, encouraging a faster walking rhythm. Wider, deeper steps tend to feel less hurried and relaxed, leading to a slower walking rhythm.
- To provide space for planted containers (on larger steps).
- To lead the user to an unexpected view or indicate a change in direction, by twisting and turning.

Another key design consideration is the style that is required. This will be influenced by several factors, including budget and client/owner preference for a formal or informal look. There may be a local historical tradition or building style. For example, Victorian style tended to have lots of straight lines and angles, giving a very formal feel. The style of a Victorian property can be successfully complemented by traditional steps of straight lines and blue bricks. The journey around the garden will be less relaxing, as the eye and brain have to work hard to navigate the sharp corners.

The garden may already have been created in a certain style, and this will influence your design choices for new steps. For example, if the style of the rest of a garden is a strong one, such as Mediterranean or contemporary, then traditional-style steps would look out of

Fig. 4.17 Wide steps for a family garden.

place. Using curves will add a more relaxed style, while a Mediterranean style could be reflected in the use of terracotta tiles. Indeed, all sorts of fashions and trends in gardening – contemporary, traditional, or a combination of the two – can be matched in your choice of various materials.

Who is going to be using the steps? In a family garden, large, wide steps with wide treads will reduce the risk of accidents for children and less mobile persons. In the garden in Fig. 4.17, much of the danger that would have been imposed by the inclusion of a retaining wall or small steps has been mitigated by the installation of large wide steps, reducing the height of any potential falls.

Materials

The choice of materials will be influenced by a number of considerations:

- Re-use/recycling: are there any materials that could be re-used/recycled on site? Can you purchase recycled materials, such as crushed concrete?
- Design concept: are the chosen materials consistent with the overall design concept, for example, contemporary materials for a contemporary step style? Cut limestone gives a slick, classic contemporary feel, whereas concrete riven slabs provide a more traditional feel.
- Commercial materials: some materials that are produced on a large-scale commercial basis, such as concrete riven slabs, are readily available and comparatively cheap, but they may compromise the integrity of the design. This is obviously a subjective decision.
- Budget: natural stone is the most expensive, but there are more reasonably priced alternatives, including reconstituted stone and concrete slabs, pavers, gravel and timber.
- Locality: if there is a local material commonly used in surrounding properties, such as Cotswold stone, using another material could make the steps look out of place.
- Personal preference: of course, personal preference varies hugely from person to person, but the final decision is down to the owner or client.
- Building style and era of the adjacent property: certain materials denote certain historical eras – for

Fig. 4.18 Traditional Cotswold-style steps.

Fig. 4.19 Contemporary-style steps.

example, blue brick is closely associated with Victorian times – so it is advisable to take this into consideration.

Stone

Stone is beautiful and hard-wearing, but it is an expensive option. There are several types, including granite, limestone, sandstone, York stone and whinstone. The different types will have differing textures and the final finish can be fine or roughly dressed.

The thickness of the stone used will have an impact on the final riser measurements. It is also possible to have stone-effect pavers made with concrete or other man-made materials, but you must check that they are suitable for outdoor steps before ordering them.

Fig. 4.20 Steps at Kailsie.

Fig. 4.21 Portland limestone.

Fig. 4.22 Natural sandstone.

Fig. 4.23 York stone.

Fig. 4.24 Steps with a gravel tread.

Gravel

There are a few potential issues to be aware of when creating steps with a gravel tread:

- Containment of the gravel: the gravel will need to be securely contained, to prevent it washing away. Often, this is done by using timber, perhaps a sleeper on its edge. This is usually suitable but, if the timber gets too wet, algae will grow on the surface, creating a slip hazard. This can be avoided either by applying a paint to which sand has been added or by attaching grip strips, which are a bit like heavy-duty sandpaper.
- Movement: the gravel can be kicked up or move underfoot. This can be avoided by using an 'angular' gravel. While round gravel will roll around, angular gravel will lock together when pressure is applied.
- Gravel heights: the level of gravel can change over time, as it is taken away on people's shoes or the gravel settles. If that happens, the edge of the tread may rise up, creating a small trip hazard.

Fig. 4.25 Brick steps at Hidcote Manor Garden in Gloucestershire.

- Colour: there are many different colours to choose from so the gravel can be selected to match or harmonize with surrounding hard landscaping.
- Cost: gravel is relatively cost-effective in comparison to slabs, bricks and pavers.
- Maintenance: the gravel will need topping up as and when required. Weed treatment will also be necessary, as seeds germinate very easily into gravel.

Brick

When choosing bricks, check whether they are suitable for use in the construction of steps – generally speaking, the harder the brick the better. In terms of design, consider the architecture and brick colour of the adjacent property or other buildings – bricks in the UK tend to be in shades of yellow and red.

There are a few potential issues to be aware of when creating steps with brick:

- Density: the bricks need to be hard-wearing and frost-proof.
- Colour: choose the colour to tie in with nearby buildings and the house. Remember that red advances and blue recedes, so the redder the brick, the more dominant the steps will appear, while the bluer/greyer the brick, the less dominant it will be.
- Construction: when brick is used for step treads there should be no wet soil in contact with the brick surface. The wet will be absorbed from the soil into the brick and, when it freezes in winter, the face of the brick will be blown off.
- Blue brick: the hardest type of brick, which tends to have a smooth surface, can be slippery in wet weather, especially if the steps are in the shade.
- Cost: brick can be fairly expensive, but they are long-lasting.
- Maintenance: very little work is required unless there is algal growth that needs to be removed.

Timber

Timber will give a very natural look to steps, so is very much in keeping with a looser, more relaxed and naturalistic garden style. It is also a cost-effective option in two ways: the materials are cheaper to buy and less labour is required to install timber steps.

There are a few potential issues to be aware of when creating steps with timber:

Fig. 4.26 Timber steps.

- Limited lifespan: although it will be treated before installation, timber will rot over time.
- Slip hazard: timbers steps will become slippery in the wet, particularly if they are in the shade and receive very little sun.
- Cost: timber is a budget-friendly option but has a comparatively short lifespan when compared with stone and brick.
- High maintenance: be aware that, if they are to remain solid and in a safe condition, timber steps will need annual maintenance work. This means regular resanding, and treating with stain and preservative. Application of algal remover may also be necessary. If you have the time and are happy to keep a close eye on the steps, this may not be an issue.

Recycled railway sleepers have been used in the past for steps, but this is now not recommended because of the levels of creosote and environmentally harmful chemicals involved, which can leach into the soil around the site.

Construction

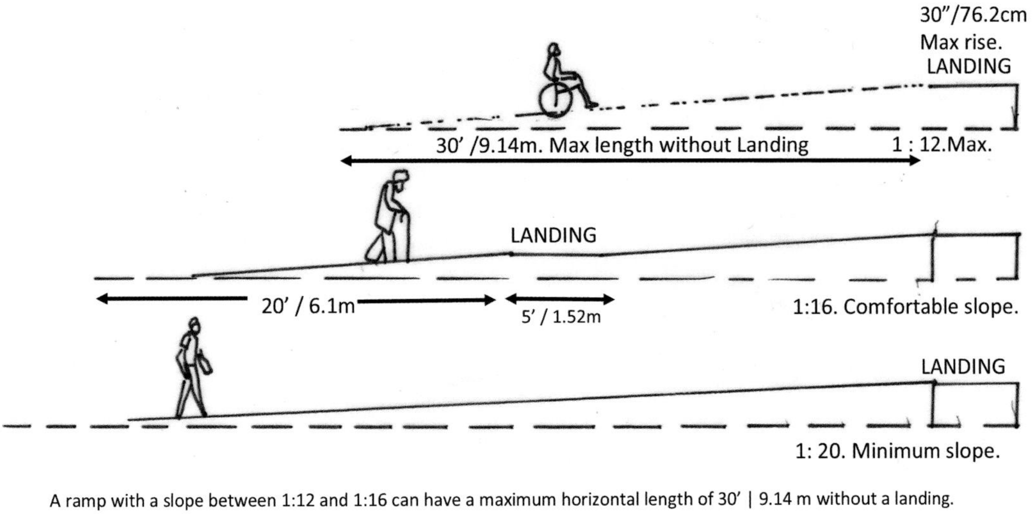

Fig. 4.27 Ramps and landings.

Fig. 4.28 The anatomy of a step.

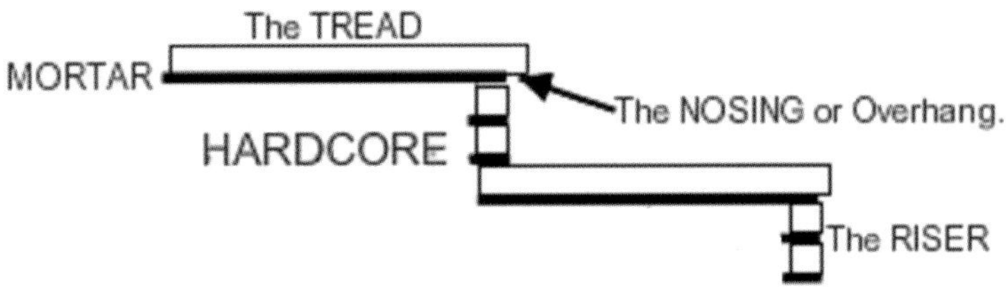

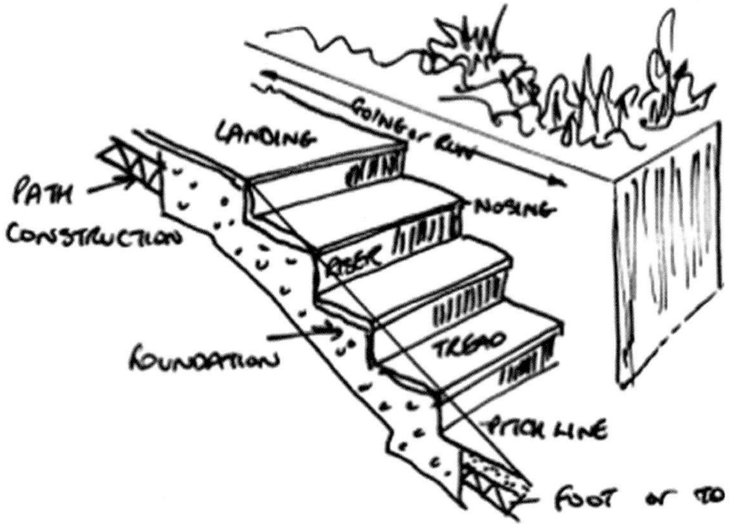

Fig. 4.29 A typical flight of steps.

The Parts of a Step

The riser is the height of the step. It should be no less than 100mm; less than 100mm is considered a trip hazard. The recommended height is 150–200mm maximum. The total height of the riser will be determined by the materials used (*see* Table 4.1).

The tread is the area that the foot goes on. It should be no less than 300mm; less than 300mm is not enough area for the full foot. The recommended depth of the tread is approximately 450mm.

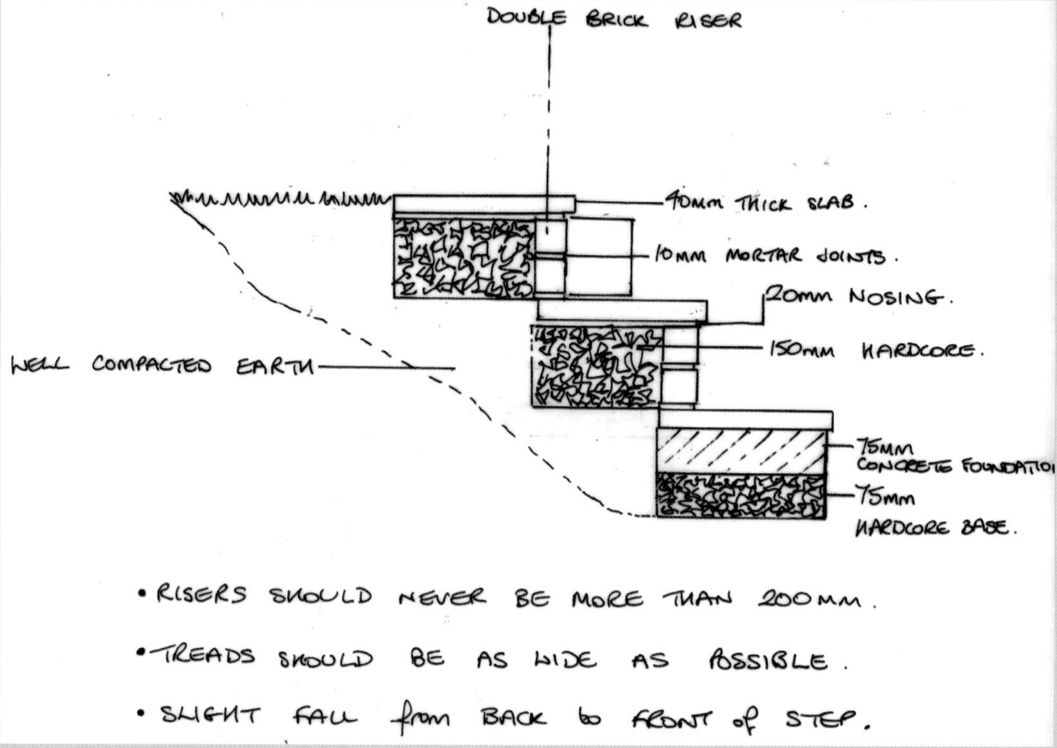

Fig. 4.30 Step construction.

Table 4.1 How step height is achieved.

Tread	40mm approx., varies from slab to slab
Mortar layer	10mm
Brick	70mm, usually varies from brick to brick
Mortar layer	10mm
Brick	70mm usually
	Total = 200mm
This is why 200mm is the max. height for each riser. The total height of the step will vary as slab and brick depths vary.	

Construction Design

The more complicated a step design, the more likely it is that you will need to seek the help of a specialist. Find a good, reliable contractor, preferably via personal recommendation, and ask to see examples of some of their work before you engage them. Large flights of steps that have integral retaining structures and use high-quality materials will need the input of a skilled contractor. Exceedingly long flights of steps and tall retaining structures may also benefit from the expert advice of a structural engineer.

There are two types of step: cut-in steps and free-standing steps. Cut-in steps are easier to construct. They are cut into the bank or slope and the earth below provides an ideal foundation. Free-standing steps are built against a vertical face and take the user from one flat level to another. It is advisable to install handrails alongside a set of free-standing steps.

When coming up with detailed plans for the construction of a set of steps, you will need to consider the following:

- How will the steps look when ascending – will they be attractive and easy to see?
- How will the steps look when descending – is there a pattern; will the outside edges and each riser edge be clear to see?
- Will the steps be clearly seen in low light?
- Will the surface texture be safe? A smooth surface slab is likely to become slippery with ice and frost, and may develop algal growth in the winter, especially in damp shady conditions.
- Will the steps be strong enough for their intended use?
- Are the height of the risers and the depth of the tread in line with current building advice?

There are a number of issues that occur fairly commonly with steps, which can compromise safety. For examples of these, *see* Figs 4.31 to 4.37.

Fig. 4.31 Timber steps may be unsafe if they are free-standing (not fixed to anything), or do not have a handrail. Large gaps between the treads could cause a trip hazard, and if the timber is untreated it will be slippery in wet weather and in winter.

Fig. 4.32 Steps of different heights at Knightshayes in Devon. They present a couple of hazards: the risers are not of a uniform height so could result in a trip, and the ivy growing across them could also cause a slip or trip.

Fig. 4.33 Poorly designed steps at Milldene. The steps are very narrow so cannot accommodate two people side by side, making assistance difficult. The very deep risers pose a trip hazard, and there are no landings, which results in too long a run for those with limited mobility.

Fig. 4.34 Steps at Bicton Park Botanical Gardens in Devon. The narrow treads mean that the foot cannot fit comfortably on the step; another issue is the lack of any landings for taking a rest.

Fig. 4.35 Steps showing algal growth on slab treads. The smooth surface of the bricks would pose a slip hazard when wet. The treads are narrow and there are no landings.

Fig. 4.36 A set of steps in the garden at Powis Castle, which are too narrow to allow two people to pass or walk side by side, and have insufficient landings. The hedge will also cause shade, causing the stone to become slippery in wet or winter weather.

Fig. 4.37 Algal growth on slab treads causes a serious slip hazard.

Notes on Construction

- Width: the steps should be wide enough to allow for the easy passage of two people side by side, or the carrying of equipment.
- Fall: it is important to design in some fall (slope) on the tread, to direct water away and to prevent any puddling on the tread. If there is any surface water on the step and it freezes, it presents a real danger to users. A fall of 1:80 is usually regarded as a minimum, so a 600mm wide step should have at least 8mm of fall, preferably 10–12mm.
- Visibility: the edges of the steps need to be clearly visible. If necessary, this can be achieved by painting them in a bright colour or by using a different-coloured material along the edge. A pale slab with a dark paver or brick edge can look very pleasing. A riser of a darker colour may also be used to define a pale slab edge.
- Height: the risers should all be the same height and no more than 200mm. Even an unexpected difference of as little as 15mm in the riser can cause people to stumble.
- Depth: the treads should all be the same depth – no less than 300mm and preferably 450mm – and should have a non-slip surface.
- Providing breaks: landings are required to provide an effective break in the run of steps for the user to take a breather. Generally, there should be a landing every four to six steps, unless the treads have been designed to be deep enough for a wheelchair user to stop safely.

Retaining Structures

Note: if the slope is steep and needs the installation of retaining structures to create flat, level areas, the likelihood is that each retaining structure will need to be more than 1.2m high, in which case a structural engineer should be involved in their design and development.

When making a slope usable and safe, steps are the obvious answer for easy access. Some slopes will be too steep to even mow and maintain, let alone garden in comfortably, in which case the slope will need to be split into a series of level areas or terraces, with retaining structures. Retaining structures are constructed for a range of purposes:

- To create raised beds.
- To act as a backdrop for a water feature.
- To create a series of level areas; this is known as terracing.

Fig. 4.38 Raised bed.

Fig. 4.39 A retaining wall used as a backing structure for a pool.

In most instances, a retaining structure is built to hold back earth and will have to withstand a significant amount of pressure, current recommendations are as follows:

- It should be at least 250mm thick.
- It should slope slightly backwards.
- It will require drainage – either weep holes or a drainage channel such as an ACO channel at the base, so water draining down the slope can escape.

Retaining structures can be constructed from bricks, blocks, stone or timber (the most frequently used materials), or concrete. Sometimes, metal is used to create a seamless look, as the top of the metal cannot be seen, unlike the top of a wall or a row of sleepers.

Fig. 4.40 Terracing.

Brick, Block, Stone or Concrete Walls

A wall will be the most expensive option in terms of both materials and labour, but it offers a number of benefits:

- Strength and durability: the most commonly used materials for a retaining wall are brick, block, stone and concrete, all of which are solid materials that provide stability and noise reduction. They may also deter people from taking a short cut over the top!
- It will require minimal maintenance.
- In terms of landscaping, it can reflect a long-term vision to enhance the environment and they look expensive.
- The structure can be designed to echo the particular style of the surrounding area, so that it sits well in its surroundings.
- Although it is the most expensive option, it will be extremely long-lasting.

Fig. 4.41 A retaining wall in cut Cotswold stone.

Fig. 4.42 Mount Stewart garden in Northern Ireland: a naturalistic retaining wall built from large chunks of stone.

Fig. 4.43 Mount Stewart garden: a wall built with gaps for 'windows'.

Fig. 4.44 Block and render retaining wall.

ABOVE AND RIGHT: Fig. 4.45 Timber retainer used to create level growing beds.

Fig. 4.46 A slope before any terracing work has been carried out.

Fig. 4.47 The slope after terracing.

Fig. 4.48 Sleepers set in concrete strip foundation.

Timber Retaining Structures

A retaining structure can equally be constructed from timber. Recycled railway sleepers are popular because of their weight, ease of construction and cost-effectiveness. This method offers a number of benefits:

- Strength and durability: the timber used for a retaining structure will be a heavy, solid material that may not need foundations if it is being laid horizontally. If a curved retaining structure is required, the timbers can be cut into shorter lengths and laid vertically into a concrete strip foundation (*see* Fig. 4.48).
- Landscaping and style: timber is a natural material that will provide a very soft, naturalistic-looking structure that will sit easily within its surrounding environment.
- A timber retaining structure will be less expensive than a wall in terms of both labour and materials.

The downside is that a timber structure will require more in terms of maintenance, with a preservative treatment of the wood every couple of years.

Timber retaining structures can also be built from logs piled on top of one another, a bit like a giant insect hotel. The logs will need to be large and heavy in order to withstand the weight of the earth behind the structure.

The considerations of design and the materials available for retaining structures are much the same as for steps. Other options available are gabions (stone-filled metal cages; *see* Fig. 4.57) and sheet metal or Corten steel.

Ramps

Ramps are not just for wheelchair users. They are increasingly being installed to provide safe and easy access to public buildings such as libraries, museums, shopping areas, and so on, for people pushing prams or pushchairs, cyclists pushing a bike, and older people using a walking stick or frame. They are also safer for children to use.

A ramp will offer a much safer option than steps to provide a smooth means of changing level and to remove the presence of a trip hazard for all users. Unfortunately, they require much more space than steps in order to produce a sufficiently gentle gradient.

Fig. 4.49 Public access steps and ramp.

There are certain construction technicalities and guidelines that need to be followed when constructing a ramp:

- Gradient: the building regulations as applied to constructing a disabled access ramp state that 'where the gradient of the approach, whether over its whole length or in part, is 1:20 or steeper, that part of the approach should be designed as ramped access.' (www.nurturegroup.co.uk/wheelchair-ramp-regulations).
- The accepted gradient for a ramp is 1:12, meaning that for every 12m travelled horizontally the level changes by 1m. This results in a workable gradient for a wheelchair user.

Consideration to the ramp dimensions is essential if it is to function successfully and safely. The manoeuvrability of the wheelchair will determine ramp widths and landings:

- Ramp length: to find the length of ramp required, the height is multiplied by the ratio. Measure the total rise and divide by the slope. In other words, if working on a 1:12 ratio, the height of the rise is multiplied by 12 to give the minimum length of the ramp. (Wheelchair-ramps.co.uk)
- Ramp widths: there should be enough space for someone to walk alongside the wheelchair; if space allows, ideally two wheelchairs should be able to pass by each other. A typical wheelchair is 90cm wide, so the recommended ramp width for one wheelchair is 1.5m. which allows for 30cm space on either side of the wheelchair. For two wheelchairs to pass, you would need 1.8m width.

Fig. 4.50 A gentle ramp for people with limited mobility.

Fig. 4.51 Ramp with handrails.

- Landings that provide space to take a breather from physical exertion are especially important to the ramp user, particular for the wheelchair 'pusher' or somebody who is pushing themselves in the wheelchair, to break a fall or change direction.
- Ramps should be no longer than 10–12m before introducing a flat landing.
- If a ramp is more than 50cm in height, handrails should be installed either side.

For more detailed information on designing and building ramps, see the websites wheelchair-ramps.co.uk/ and nurturegroup.co.uk/wheelchair-ramp-regulations, as well as Part M of 'Building Regulations for Ramps'.

In a garden with a steeper slope, the ramp will become a major structural element. It will take up a significant amount of space as, generally speaking, it will have to 'traverse' the slope (run across it) in order to reduce the gradient. To avoid it over-dominating the look and feel of the garden, wherever possible planted areas should be included on one or both sides. These will not only counterbalance and soften the structure but will also encourage the user to stop and enjoy the plants along the way making for a pleasurable journey through the garden.

In recent years, there has been an increase in awareness of the need to facilitate easier access in both the domestic garden and in public outdoor spaces. As a result, ramps will continue to be an increasingly common feature of domestic housing, public buildings and outdoor spaces.

Changes of Level for Increased Interest

A flat garden may be easier to maintain, but it can be lacking in interest or any element of surprise, especially if all of it can be seen at once. There is no sense of adventure or motivation to explore further, to find those parts that are not immediately visible. This can be resolved by introducing more interest through small changes of level. Various elements can be created by building up or digging down, including raised beds (*see* Fig. 4.52). Another option might be to use the excavated soil from digging out a pond to form a mound at the back of it (*see* Fig. 4.53), or to create a larger raised area with a change of level (*see* Fig. 4.54).

Fig. 4.52 Raised beds creating a change of level.

In the case of the raised area in Fig. 4.54, a slight slope (about 400mm COL from patio to hedge line) was regraded. The soil was redistributed to create a split level, transforming the garden into a more interesting space with upper and lower levels. The upper level is now a flat lawn that is easy to mow, and can be used for sitting out, while the lower level is patio; the two distinct, very usable areas are linked by a small lavender-flanked pathway.

In essence, when working on a sloping site the size and gradient of the slope will determine what needs to be done. If the slope is steep, the garden will at the very least need a level pathway that 'traverses' the slope (*see* Fig. 4.55). If it is planted with grass, this can be installed in a cost-effective way and maintained without too much effort.

Fig. 4.53 A waterfall created from excavated soil.

Fig. 4.54 Split levels.

The slope of the Italian olive grove on the side of a mountain in Fig. 4.55 presented quite a challenge, but clever design and terracing allowed flat areas to be created. These act as both pathways and as planted areas and are wide enough to be mown.

A pathway that traverses the slope will almost certainly need steps included where it turns a corner at the end of each terrace.

At its most extreme, a steeply sloping garden will need split levelling, which will involve the installation of retaining structures to create several terraces, linked by steps and landings (*see* Fig. 4.56).

Working with a sloping garden is a challenge that brings with it a range of options, and requires many decisions to be made, and it can be a daunting task. As always, the best way to approach the challenge is to follow a process, working through the main factors that will affect your choices and decisions:

- Budget: this determines whether a simple or more complex design is required, or feasible.
- Style: this ensures that the various elements fit in with the property and surrounding environment. The right choice of materials is an important part of this.
- Design: this ensures an aesthetically pleasing final product.

Fig. 4.55 Pathways used as terracing.

This way of working breaks the task down into 'bite-sized' pieces, making the whole project seem more achievable. A series of logical decisions can be made for each item based on their individual merits.

Whether flat or sloping, a garden is an ever-evolving, living, natural environment that will carry on changing from year to year. A shrub that was two feet high when planted may grow to be twice as tall, and may need moving as it begins to overshadow and obscure the shorter plants behind it. As time moves forward, the ways in which the garden is used will also change. There will always be elements that could be improved, but hopefully this will mean adding to the garden rather than completely re-doing structural items. Extra time taken in the planning will always be time well spent, resulting in a garden that will remain more than satisfactory for its owner and users for many years to come.

Fig. 4.56 Gabions.

Fig. 4.57 Steel lawn edging.

CHAPTER 5

ESTABLISHING A SLOPING GARDEN

The process of creating, making and establishing a garden, like making a piece of art, a cake or a building, takes time. First, there is the seed of an idea, which, as it is worked on, grows and evolves into the final piece. Unlike most pieces of art, cakes or buildings, a garden, whether sloping or flat, is a living sculpture, which changes and evolves as the years go by. Some plants will grow too big, overshadowing other elements of the garden, and other plants will die, leaving empty spaces that need filling. As the designer's ideas come into reality they may not end up quite as they were originally envisaged. The establishment of a garden is a process during which it will develop and change every year, over the years. It will be inspired by garden programmes, plant catalogues and your own successes or failures. As much as you plan to make changes in order to create your vision of the perfect final garden, it never seems to be quite so simple.

Fig. 5.1 The spectacular open-air Minack Theatre in Cornwall.

A sloping site can be a huge challenge, yet it will offer some distinctive design opportunities, so it is a challenge that is worth taking on. For the larger

Fig. 5.2 Garden slope rising away from the house.

sloping garden, the challenge will extend over a period of time, thus reducing its intensity in terms of costs, time and energy.

If the slope rises up, away from the house, it will give a strong sense of enclosure, privacy and safety within – with the added bonus that most of the garden will be visible from the lower level. For purely practical purposes, the patio will more than likely be at house level, with the garden rising upwards away from it. It may feel as though you are in a sunken garden – and what a great dynamic this is to have. Excavating tonnes of soil to create a sunken garden would cost a fortune, yet the site is offering you a ready-made one, with the sense of being an amphitheatre. The garden surrounds and protects the user and provides a real wow factor.

Conversely, if the garden slopes downwards, away from the house, that will create a strong sense of intrigue and adventure, drawing you into the garden to explore the secrets that are hidden from view from the house. Again, for practical reasons the patio is more than likely to be immediately outside the rear doors, with steps leading off down the slope.

In order to establish either type of sloping garden, it is vital to focus on some specific factors, which may be organized under certain headings:

- Design opportunities.
- What to look out for.
- Soil: assessment of type, erosion and management.
- Drainage: does the slope require a drainage system? If so, what type?
- Water: saving, collection and reusing.
- Maintenance.
- Planting *(see* Chapters 6, 7 and 8).

Design Opportunities

Terracing

Depending on how extensive the slope is, the creation of one or more flat areas, each level accessed by steps, and separated and supported by retaining structures, maximizes the 'kerb appeal' of the site and improves its functionality. This method can be used whether the slope is towards or away from the house, with each offering a completely different result.

Terracing provides the perfect opportunity to introduce defined zones within each flat area:

Fig. 5.3 Retaining wall water feature.

- A play area on one terrace. If it is at the bottom of the slope, it could even be arrived at by a zip line.
- A kitchen garden on another, with a greenhouse.
- Outdoor dining or living spaces on another level. Transporting food and drinks is obviously much easier the nearer to the house these areas are, but secondary seating areas can be situated further away from the house.

Terraced areas can be created in either a flat or a sloping garden, but the journey between them in a sloping garden is so much more interesting, as you move from one area to the next and each one offers a different view.

Water Features

Water features may include a garden-length stream that cascades into a pool, repeated on several levels, or a waterfall or a retaining wall with water spouts. The sight and sound of falling water will bring intrigue and fascination into a garden, attract birds to drink nd provide the perfect spot to sit, in a relaxing ambience.

Fig. 5.4 Stream falling into a pool.

Concealment

A steep downhill slope means that very little, if any, of the garden can be seen from the property. This provides an ideal opportunity to hide utility structures, such as sheds and storehouses.

Focal Point

A steep uphill slope offers the opportunity to position a summerhouse or barbecue hut in full view of the house, creating an area of special interest. This can be a specific destination for outdoor entertainment, which, if surrounded by gorgeous planting, will have the look and feel of a secluded outdoor room.

Feature Steps

Large curving steps, almost amphitheatre like, whether rising up from the house, or descending down from the house, will give a sense of the garden wrapping its arms around its visitors.

What to Look Out For

Before embarking on any plans, you need to get to know the space well. This is done by identifying the following:

- The sunny and shady sides, in order to inform plant choice.
- Soil type, to indicate soil prep required and inform plant choice.
- Position of functional features such as steps, patios, and so on, for most effective use.
- Position of any structures such as a summerhouse or barbecue hut.
- Type of plants that grow in the garden naturally.
- Which mature trees and shrubs in situ already (if any) to retain, and which to remove. It is worth taking time over this – a shrub that is bare and twiggy-looking in winter can be a real asset in spring and summer, when it is in full leaf and in flower.
- The steepness of the slope – this will influence your decision as to whether you want to invest in the costly steps and terracing approach. Can you spread the costs over time, allowing you to work to a more generous budget?

Fig. 5.5 Amphitheatre-style steps.

Soil

Protection and Stabilization of Soil

If the slope is less than 33 per cent, the soil can be protected and stabilized by using a mulch. This will help to protect it from degradation by wind and weather, keep it in place and retain moisture by preventing surface evaporation. If the slope is steeper than this, there needs to be careful consideration of how accessible it is and therefore how much planting can be done in view of the maintenance requirements. Plant roots will stabilize soil on a slope.

The presence of bald spots on a sloping property can indicate a number of issues with the soil quality. For example, it may be that the grass is excessively fertilized and poorly irrigated. If the grass is very mossy, this can reflect an excess of moisture and shade. When it is raked out, bald patches may be left. Bald spots can also be a sign of bedrock and/or lots of stones just below the soil surface.

If you intend to use cover vegetation to stabilize the soil, you will need to ensure that the plants will thrive in either sun or shade. This is one reason why you need to identify the sunny and shady areas early on, so that you can select plants accordingly for the particular conditions.

Based on an assessment of these factors and the degree of the slope, it may be necessary to work with a landscaper or construction specialist for hard landscaping, and to seek professional advice with regard to plant selection. Checking off these points will ensure the smooth establishment of a sloping garden. Identifying the quality of the land you are working with will help to clarify the best methods to be employed to resolve any issues with a particular site.

Assessing Soil Structure and Composition

Soil is the life blood of any garden, providing nutrients and retaining moisture, to allow plants to produce roots for anchorage and thence to thrive. It is home to many insects, small beasts and micro-organisms, which all contribute to a healthy growing environment. The myriad creatures feed on dead leaves and other green waste products that sit on the soil surface, and their activity and the waste they produce then create the structure of the soil and the goodness found within it. Growing fruit and vegetables in soil arguably results in a much tastier product than using modern technological methods such as hydroponics, which allows plants to be grown in water that is constantly infused with nutrients. Although strawberries may now be available all year round, surely nothing compares to the flavour of a piece of fruit grown in a local field and picked at the height of summer.

To begin an assessment of the soil on the site, first have a look at its depth. Is the topsoil thin, lying mostly on top of rock and stones, or is there a good depth of topsoil supported by a thick layer of subsoil? Dig out a hole a couple of feet deep, so you can see the layers. This is to get a sense of whether any plants that are put into the existing soil will be able to take root and thrive. If not, soil prep will be necessary (*see* below). Good plant establishment should take place in about six weeks.

Soil Types

According to the RHS, there are six main soil types in the UK, each with their own characteristics:

- Clay: heavy, high in nutrients, wet and cold in winter and baked hard and dry in summer.
- Sandy: Light, dry, warm, low in nutrients and often acidic.
- Silt: fertile, light but moisture-retentive, easily compacted.
- Loams: mixtures of clay, sand and silt that avoid the extremes of each type.
- Peat: high in organic matter and moisture-retentive.
- Chalk: very alkaline and may be light or heavy.

Basically, it is the size of the soil particles that differentiate each soil type and how they each perform in terms of water retention and nutrient-holding properties, and in terms of their vulnerability or resistance to soil erosion.

The two most common soil types in the UK are clay and sandy soils.

Clay Soils

- Problems: clay soils present a number of problems. They have low absorption rates – they are very slow to absorb water, so water will be seen 'puddling' on the surface. The soil particles cling firmly to each other, making the soil very sticky when wet. Clay soils can still be easily eroded by water but seem to be more durable against wind.

- Nutrient levels: a clay soil is nutritious but its capacity to hold water can become a major problem in winter, when plant roots sit in water for weeks and literally drown.
- Solution: the addition of well-rotted compost (manure is too sticky) and fine sharp horticulture grit will help to open the soil up, to improve aeration and drainage. This will provide a softer medium that can be penetrated more easily by the plants' roots.

Sandy/Silty Soils

- Problems: the particles in sandy/silty soils are loose and movable, so the sandier a soil is, the easier it is for water, wind and snow to make off with it. It is completely the opposite to clay soil, where the soil particles stick together. Sandy/silty soils are more stable if they are covered in dense vegetation.
- Nutrient levels: the soft, fine texture of a sandy/silty soil allows for the quick establishment of a plant root system. The downside is that water very quickly soaks through it, taking the soil's nutrients with it. This results in a soil of poor or low nutrition as well as low moisture, causing the plants to dry out very quickly.
- Solution: to prevent plants suffering from malnutrition, this type of soil needs the regular addition of compost and well-rotted manure to improve its structure and water retention, and increase nutrient levels. An annual mulch of tree bark will reduce the rate of surface evaporation and improve moisture levels.

Soil Erosion

Preventing soil erosion on a hillside is quite a challenge. Sloping sites come in many different shapes and sizes and it is the topography of the particular slope, along with any sloping surrounding land, that will determine the method that will be necessary to prevent soil erosion. If the slope is gentle, major soil erosion issues are less likely to occur and planting alone can be a cost-effective way to stabilize the soil surface.

Sandy soils are more prone to run-off than soils with a clay make-up because the particles in sandy soils are looser. Rainfall causes surface run-off, which produces three main types of soil erosion:

- Splash erosion: splash or raindrop impact is the first stage in the erosion process. Splash erosion results from the weight of the impact on the soil surface of falling raindrops.
- Sheet erosion: this occurs when soil is washed away in thin layers by rainwater that does not soak into the ground but runs across the surface.
- Rill erosion and gully erosion: rill erosion is when run-off water forms small channels as it runs down a slope. A rill can be up to 0.3mm deep; it is considered to be a gully when it becomes deeper than this.

In a nutshell, erosion is caused by the weather, which has become so variable in recent years, with more frequent episodes of extreme weather, particularly periods of heavy rainfall and more severe strong winds. The result has been soil erosion problems that have probably not been experienced in the average garden before.

The elements can have a number of detrimental effects on a garden:

- Wind: light soil is dried out and surface soil can then be blown away; heavy soil is dried out, making the surface hard and cracked.
- Heavy rain: light soil will be washed away over time; on heavy soil, it can cause flooding due to slow or no water absorption; soil compaction may be caused by the surface impact of heavy raindrops.
- Snow: even light snow that has settled can slip, taking soil with it; on heavy soil, snow settled on the surface can cause compaction and waterlogging.

Management

Once you have identified the soil type or types, it will be possible to determine what action needs to be taken to manage and mitigate the problems (*see* Table 5.1).

Controlling Soil Erosion

Soil erosion is easier to control these days thanks to the availability of a vastly increased selection of mate-

Table 5.1 Problems and solutions according to soil type

PROBLEMS	ACTION
Free-draining sandy soil	
Structure needs improvement and 'bulking up'	Add well-rotted compost and manure, and leaf mould if available
Moisture retention needs improvement	Use membrane and mulch to reduce evaporation from surface
Lack of moisture	Water frequently, daily in summer, at the base of plants
Low nutrient levels	Feed often with slow-release granules and occasional liquid feed
Clay soil	
Structure needs opening up	Add horticultural grit at rate of 1 bucket per sq m and incorporate loose, dry compost
Drainage needs improving	Use tree bark mulch, which will break down over time and improve soil structure. Do not use membrane
Retains too much moisture	Do not over-water. Water every two to three days in summer, at the base of plants
Occasional low nutrient levels	Observe plants for any deficiency and feed when appropriate
Other notes on soil care	
Autumn leaves	Can be collected and left through winter to create leaf mould. Do not leave on clay soil as they will hold water on the surface
Autumn die-back, both soil types	Dead leaves and stems that have been cut back can be chopped up and left on soil surface as natural mulch, or left as a wildlife habitat and food source until spring cut-back
Bulb planting, on clay soil	Place 20mm of horticulture grit in base of planting hole, to prevent bulbs sitting in water
Manure	Not suitable for use on clay soil as its sticky nature will make the 'clods' worse

rials and construction methods. The main techniques are:

- Building terracing.
- Using sandbags to create diversions. Although it is difficult to fight against nature, as a temporary measure you can try to channel and divert it until a more permanent solution can been found.
- Stabilization using geotextiles or erosion-control blankets.
- Stabilization with planting.

Controlling Erosion on Clay Soil

Whatever the soil type, using plants to cover the area is the best way to control erosion. Selecting the right plants is key to success and dependent upon how steep or shallow the slope is. You may need to find a temporary solution such as membrane and mulch, to hold it in place while the plants become established.

The right plants for a clay-based soil must like a dense structure (a very cloddy structure can be broken down with soil prep; *see* Table 5.1) and moisture-reten-

Fig. 5.6 Pre-seeded erosion-control blanket.

Fig. 5.7 Terram geocell slope-erosion control.

Fig. 5.8 Anchoring solutions for soil stabilization.

Fig. 5.9 A sandy gully with soil-erosion control.

tive soil, and must be able to tolerate wet soil during winter.

In terms of structure, you may decide to introduce some channels at intervals across the slope to collect and interrupt water run-off as it travels down the slope, thereby reducing soil collected on its journey. Alternatively, terracing can be used to create flat surfaces that will not be subject to water run-off.

Controlling Erosion on Sandy/Silty Soil

The sandier a soil is, with loose and movable particles, the easier it is for water, wind and snow to make off with it. Such soils are very fine and erode easily if they are not covered in dense vegetation.

The soft, fine texture of sandy and silty soils facilitates the quick establishment of plants. However, water very quickly soaks through them, taking nutrients with it, resulting in the plants suffering from malnutrition. The right plants for a sandy-based soil must be able to get on with low levels of nutrition. They will need to be drought-tolerant and to self-seed easily.

In terms of structural elements, you can use erosion-control textiles – the pre-seeded versions would be excellent on this type of soil. Terracing and retaining structures will hold soil back, preventing erosion, and gabions and drystone walling can be crevice planted. Brick, stone or timber walls can incorporate raised beds that maximize growing conditions for plants.

Fig. 5.10 A swale, installed to provide drainage to a housing estate.

Drainage

There is a simple test for measuring the drainage on a hillside:

1. Dig a hole and fill it with water.
2. After an hour or two, check back. If there is no water lingering, the natural drainage is good.
3. If after two or more days the water is still sitting there, that means there is rock and/or heavy clay beneath any topsoil, both of which are largely water resistant. In this case, any planting areas on the slope will need good soil preparation (*see* Table 5.1)

Waterlogging can be prevented by means of soil improvement, but this can take some time as it will be necessary to wait for the soil structure to change, therefore posing a threat to any new planting. The alternative is to install a drainage system. There are several forms to choose from and your choice will depend on the size of the slope being dealt with:

- Swales: natural or man-made linear channels in the soil, usually covered with grass, with shallow-sloping sides. They can be planted up. They are commonly used in commercial settings to direct surface water run-off away from properties, pathways and roads. This method can be used on a smaller scale in an individual setting, for example, at the bottom of a slope.
- Ditches: a ditch differs from a swale in that its sides are not usually grass covered. They are usually installed in a rural environment, to take surface-water run-off from fields.
- French drain: a trench, part-filled with aggregate through which runs a slotted plastic pipe, that redirects subsoil and water away from the garden and/or property in areas that are prone to flooding or surface water pooling. For example, a property surrounded by higher land which slopes towards the

Fig. 5.11 A French drain.

property. and garden. The ditch is dug with a sloping base which runs in a direction away from the property. Before installing a French drain, it is advisable to take expert advice, it is important to avoid any buried pipes, cables or other installations.

- ACO channel: a system that involves a linear plastic channel (a bit like plastic guttering) which is installed below the surface level, at the edge of the surface to be drained. A slotted plastic grid clips on the top to prevent it filling up with dead leaves and other debris. The hard surface will have a slight slope which directs surface water run-off towards the ACO channel, which then runs into a storm water drain.
- Gravel channel: a small trench approximately 8–10 inches (20–25cm) deep and 8–10 inches wide, installed along the base of a retaining structure (commonly seen around house perimeters) where the house line is lower than that of the surrounding areas. It collects the water as it drains down the slope. This method can be repeated on each level of a split-levelled sloping garden.

Fig. 5.12 Aco drainage channel.

Fig. 5.13 ACO channel for a driveway.

Fig. 5.14 Gravel drainage channel.

Water

It seems appropriate to discuss water conservation alongside drainage, particularly as a sloping site offers natural drainage, which can be harnessed to create an irrigation system for the garden. Water is a precious commodity and in the face of a changing climate, with issues such as prolonged drought on one hand and flash flooding on the other, it is vital to keep as much of your natural water resource – rainfall – as you can within the garden. Flash flooding occurs when existing elderly drainage systems cannot cope with sudden, heavy rainfall. A further major contributory factor is the ever-increasing amount of hard surface in front gardens, built to slope towards the road. In addition, there has been the significant loss of so much green space to the construction of housing developments, with their hard surface roads, driveways and roofs. The increased rainfall drains off the hard surfaces into roadside storm water systems that do not have sufficient capacity for the quantities involved. In fact, flooding has become such an issue of late that developers now have to submit detailed storm water drainage systems as part of their planning consent application. Driveways have to be surfaced with semi-permeable materials and often an ACO channel is required across the boundary to collect storm water run-off that would otherwise run into the roadside system.

This modern-day issue has been intensely researched by UK-based Dr Nigel Dunnet from Sheffield University, who is renowned for his work on sustainable planting, converting grey/brown sites to green, and water conservation, among other topics. He has studied methods of keeping storm water run-off immediately local, recycling it onsite via an irrigation system, not just in the immediate environment on large projects but also within private gardens. He has also pioneered the installation of green roofs as a way of controlling the temperature in towns and cities, and reinstating the green footprint of any building. These topics, along with those of living walls and sustainable planting, are covered in his book *Rain Gardens: Managing Water Sustainably in the Garden and Designed Landscape*, which is highly recommended.

Fig. 5.15 A green roof.

The concept of the rain garden may seem eclectic but it can be relevant for any private site. A sloping garden demands considerable increased effort in terms of watering, but this can be offset by employing some very practical and attractive solutions to maximize the use of water collected from rainfall onsite:

- Reduce erosion by creating rainfall collection pools that are connected with small streams or cascades, controlling the way in which the water moves around the site.
- Create rainfall collection pools for watering.

Fig. 5.16 Sustainable planting at Trentham Gardens, near Stoke-on-Trent.

Fig. 5.17 Living wall at Yorkshire Artspace.

A slope offers the ideal opportunity to implement sustainable water-collecting and water-saving methods. The collected water can then be used for onsite watering, reducing the amount that needs to be taken from the mains water supply. These water-saving solutions can also help with some other potential issues that come to mind. First, how is the planted slope going to be watered? On a smaller site, the average hose will be long enough to reach, but in a larger garden, the watering process will involve the unwinding and rewinding of long lengths of hose. This could be mitigated by having multiple outdoor taps installed around the slope, but this would involve additional work and inconvenience. Using precious water supplies is not sustainable during times of prolonged dry spells, and possibly hosepipe bans, so it is vital to consider one or more of the water-saving solutions.

Where a large sloping area needs regular watering, an irrigation system run from a water collection vessel with a pump, the installation of dipping tanks and water collection pools – all will provide water sources around the slope. Part of the answer to this issue lies in selecting the right plants for the soil type and aspect, to reduce watering requirements.

Irrigation is an absolute necessity for the establishment of healthy new planting. The emphasis is on 'healthy' – the aim is for the plants to thrive not just survive.

The saving, collection and reuse of water is a fascinating and broad subject, much of which is relevant to the sloping garden. In the interest of creating a sustainable garden and making the most of your natural water resources, it is important to try to employ at least a few of the water-saving methods.

- Position water butts or dipping tanks around the slope so that only short walks are necessary to fill watering cans.
- Use 'leaky hoses' positioned in key areas of planting, connected to a large water collection vessel.

The emphasis is on making the most of the rainwater that falls on the garden and the wider landscape by capturing, channelling and diverting it within the garden. The following features will all be useful – and some may also contribute aesthetically to the garden:

- Green roofs: can be installed on any garden structure and will drastically reduce water run-off.
- Green walls: if the retaining structure is of gabions or drystone walling, crevice planting will increase water absorption.
- Water collection raised planters: raised beds planted with moisture-loving plants into which the higher levels drain.
- Small swales: can run along the base of retaining structures or several can run across the site and at the bottom of a slope.
- Roof water run-off downpipes: can be positioned to drain into a small pool or raised planter.
- Water butts: can be installed to collect storm water.
- Rain-chains: can divert rainwater from a gutter directly into the ground.

Maintenance

All planting schemes need regular maintenance and the flatter the garden the easier it is. Clearly, maintaining a sloping site that has not been modified will be physi-

Fig. 5.18 Planting through a membrane.

Fig. 5.19 Watering with drip irrigation on a slope.

cally more demanding than looking after a slope that has been reduced. The main maintenance tasks are weeding, watering, pruning and nutrition.

Weeding

Laying a weed-suppressant membrane secured with large pins, through which plants are planted, and finishing with a mulch can almost eliminate the need for weeding.

There are of course deep-rooted perennial weeds, such as couch grass and ground elder, which are exceptionally difficult to eradicate completely. If weeds like these are present on the site, you will need to invest time and energy into a weed treatment programme prior to any planting. This would involve spraying with a systemic weedkiller directly on to the foliage, and waiting a couple of weeks for it to be absorbed into the roots. Any new growth is then re-treated and the process is repeated until no regrowth appears and the soil is clean.

Watering

Water needs to be delivered to the base of a plant to ensure thorough wetting of the root ball. Depending on how many plants require watering it may be wise to invest in a drip irrigation system. Even if the plants are tough shrubs or drought-tolerant, they still require water to become established. Crafting channels for water flow through the root system, whether by hose or rainfall, is also a successful solution.

Fig. 5.20 Tiered irrigation channel.

Pruning

The physical demands of the task of pruning will depend on the number and size of plants that need it, and on the topography of the site. Inevitably, the flatter the ground for standing on is, the easier it is to prune and the safer it is for ladders. The transport and disposal of all the prunings is also a necessary task and wheelbarrows do not balance very well on a slope. Using evergreens can reduce or resolve this issue completely, as the prunings can be chipped in situ and then used as a mulch. This modern-day labour-saving method is increasingly commonly used.

Nutrition

A plant's requirement for nutrition is much more significant when it is growing in a fine soil. Ongoing maintenance of the garden can include the application of a mulch of well-rotted compost and manure, which will break down into the soil over time. Autumn/winter is the optimum time for this task. Other than that, sprinkling over a slow-release granular feed in spring and late summer will ensure a supply of nutrients to plants over several months. If any plants look sick, a liquid feed can be used to provide a quick tonic.

Timescale

Due to the increased costs of developing a sloping garden, the timescale to establish it may be somewhat longer than for a flat garden. This can be seen in a positive light, in that it allows extra time to get to know the space and to identify any particular likes and dislikes relating to the slope. You may notice a striking viewpoint from a particular position, where a lovely seating area could be created from which to enjoy the view. There may be trees or large shrubs that block a nice view or conversely an ugly view that needs to be screened. The ultimate aim is the establishment of an ideal sloping garden that functions at its best, looks beautiful and, despite the initial challenges, is a green space that provides a sense of enjoyment and relaxation.

CHAPTER 6

PLANNING THE PLANTING SCHEME

Plants are the essence of any garden. They 'flesh out' and soften the structure or 'bones' of the hard landscaping and will create a particular mood and/or convey a specific style, depending upon which are chosen. All gardens have a character that is derived from the way their structure and plants are linked together. How different the still, mysterious feel of a dark, shady woodland is from the light, uplifting aspect of a sunny, flowery meadow. These are the kinds of mood that can be recreated through plant selection. Of course, the key consideration in attempting to evoke a particular atmosphere is matching the plants to the specific growing conditions.

The main factors to consider when planning a plant-

Fig. 6.1 Planting on a slope at the Eden Project in Cornwall.

ing scheme will be covered in different sections in this chapter. Those factors (and sections) are as follows:

- site conditions;
- plant establishment;
- style or theme;
- plant selection;
- maintenance;
- budget.

Site Conditions

Identifying the conditions of the site is an extremely important aspect of the planning process for a planting scheme. Planning the planting for a sloping area starts with an evaluation of the slope and its pitch and the quantity of run-off. This will give direction as to the favoured method to manage the slope. There are four options:

- Terracing: if the slope is more than 30 degrees, terracing may be the better option, to prevent topsoil erosion and the escape of all moisture down the slope every time you water, or it rains.
- Groundworks: to remodel the slope.
- Planting: to stabilize the slope.
- A combination of the above, for example, terracing and planting, groundworks and planting, and so on.

As the living element of the garden, plants must have their individual needs taken into account if a healthy planted slope is to be established. Just like humans, plants have various requirements in terms of nutrition and hydration – these are referred to by gardeners as soil, moisture and feeding. Also like humans, for whom differing dietary and environmental requirements are beneficial to healthy development, plants will fail to grow and thrive if their needs are not met. In order to develop a beautiful, healthy eco-habitat, a gardener will need a good knowledge of the right conditions and requirements. Acquiring a working knowledge of plant biology, the growth habits of plants, their needs, their life cycles and the habitats in which they grow quite naturally can take years, but it will help you understand how to care for them.

Thanks to technology, it is possible to carry out detailed research via a vast range of books, online videos, podcasts and articles, to ensure the plants chosen will suit the specific growing environment. It is most important for the amateur to do a decent amount of research before selecting the plants and certainly, to avoid expensive failures, before purchasing them. Garden centre labelling can be somewhat generic and is not always accurate – be wary of a conifer that is labelled as 'dwarf', but may grow to more than 2 metres!

Of course, one way of taking a shortcut through this lengthy research process is to use the services of a professional garden designer. However, if you want to start the process yourself, you first need to make an assessment of the site conditions.

Soil

First and foremost, establishing a successful new planting scheme – meaning strong, healthy plants that are thriving, not just surviving – requires attention to the very foundation of any garden: the soil. The first step is to assess the soil and determine what type it is (*see* Chapter 5). Once the soil type has been identified, other tasks will need to be carried out to prepare the ground. These may include weed clearance, specific soil preparation, such as adding horticulture grit and well-rotted compost to clay soil to improve drainage, and the laying of membrane if appropriate. These tasks should be carried out in this logical order in readiness for planting.

It is of paramount importance to know the soil type of the site in order to select the right plants. For example, a moisture-retentive soil will best suit plants such as Hostas, Astilbes, Hydrangeas, Ligularia, Eupatoria and Dicentra (*see* Chapter 8). The approach of 'right plant, right place' is key to the establishment of a planting scheme that is not only beautiful but also healthy. A healthy planting scheme requires less maintenance as its plants should have optimum resistance to disease and pests.

If the soil has been covered with rough grass, has been heavily cultivated or is a fine, free-draining soil, then it is highly likely to be deficient in nutrients. This problem can be resolved by importing and incorporating a mix of topsoil, soil conditioner and compost to improve moisture retention. This in turn will enable more nutrients to be retained (*see* Table 5.1).

Water and Drainage

If a plant is sitting in wet, soggy soil, it will be unable to develop a healthy root system. The tiny, fine rootlets through which water, oxygen and nutrients are carried to the main body of the plant will rot. Starved of these essential elements, the plant will become stressed and eventually die. A sure sign of waterlogging is surface puddling, which often has a stagnant water odour.

If waterlogging is likely to be a problem, it will be necessary to install a drainage system prior to embarking on any soil prep. The type of system will be dependent upon the extent of the slope and water content of the soil.

At the opposite end of the scale, a steep slope will drain very quickly, resulting in a hard, dry soil and the same effect of inadequate, if any, root development.

Aspect

The slope will face in a certain direction – indeed, in a large garden, there may be a number of areas all facing in different directions – and it is important to ascertain how much or how little sun each area to be planted will receive. Plants may then be chosen according to their sun and shade requirements, as well as all the other growing conditions. It is well worth taking the time to work this out, to avoid the disappointment of a flowering plant not flowering due to lack of light or too much exposure to sun. A sun-loving plant will not thrive in shade, and will produce rather anaemic-looking straggly growth as it seeks more light.

The four main aspects in the UK are:

- north-facing: very little sun, partial shade to deep shade;
- south-facing: sun, hot, no shade, dry;
- east-facing: morning sun, shady after about 11am;
- west-facing: evening sun, shady most of the day.

There are further variables in between the main aspects – NW, NE, SW and SE – which are broadly described as having degrees of light or partial shade and light or full sun. The other factor to bear in mind when thinking about sunny and shady areas is the position of the sun at different times of the year. During the summer months it is higher in the sky and then it has a lower trajectory during the winter. When it comes to the planning of planting, getting to know a site and its particular nuances over a period of time, maybe even a full four seasons, is extremely useful.

Plant Establishment and Care

Developing a healthy planting scheme involves much more than simply putting a plant into the soil. As long as it is the right plant for the particular type of soil, and time and energy have been invested in good soil preparation and in ensuring an adequate watering system, it should establish within a six-week period.

Roots

The first process in the establishment of any plant is the development of a strong root system. Not all plants have the same type of root system. Broadly speaking, trees and shrubs develop longer, deeper roots – being much larger plants, they need good anchorage – as

Fig. 6.2 The first soft roots put out by the plant.

Fig. 6.3 Microrrhizal fungi.

well as a finer fibrous root system for the transport of food and water. Perennials develop more fibrous roots for the supply of their food and water.

Once it has been put in the soil, a garden-ready plant will spend about the first six weeks (roughly speaking) of its life developing a root system outside of its original root ball that formed in the pot. Known as 'fibrous roots', these are very fine and soft, so it is important to provide them with a loose, soft growing medium that is easily penetrated. This stage is crucial to the long-term health and vitality of the plant. As well as providing a suitable growing medium, root development and establishment may also be encouraged by the use of a product called mycorrhizal fungi.

Mycorrhizae are found in soil and create a beneficial relationship between specialized fungi and plants. The fungi colonize the root system of the plant and stimulate increased water and nutrient absorption, which encourages root growth. in the meantime, the plant provides the fungus with carbohydrates formed from photosynthesis, so each supports the other. Mycorrhizal fungi can be purchased in powder and granular form from most garden centres or online. When trying to establish new plants, it is well worth using, especially if the growing conditions are challenging.

Healthy roots are fundamental to the survival of a plant, but these unseen structures perform another role in the sloping garden. Roots not only provide the plant with the basic elements of food and water but also, on a sloping site, a good strong root system serves to anchor the plant. This in turn assists in stabilizing the soil and therefore can be a significant factor in reducing soil erosion on a sloping site.

Shoots

Once any moisture retention and erosion problems have been resolved, it is time to further evaluate the site for exposure and zone (frost exposure levels), to give the new plants every chance of survival. Plants have differing resistance levels to frost, known as 'hardiness'. If a plant will survive through the winter months in the UK it is described as 'hardy'; if it will not, then it is known as 'tender' and it will need protection such as a greenhouse for the coldest months of the year. The UK is divided into 'hardiness' zones – further south it is warmer and further north it is colder. Gardeningknow-

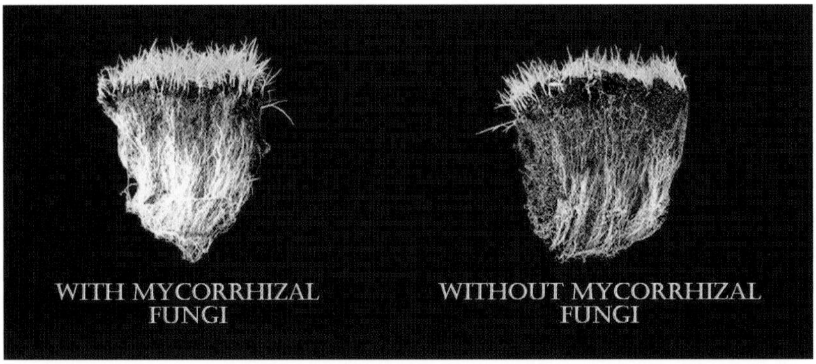

Fig. 6.4 Differences in root growth.

how.com-planting zones is an excellent website to see a hardiness map and determine which area the site is located in. Generally speaking, you would select hardy plants for a permanent planting scheme.

Feeding

Good soil prep will provide for the plants' feeding requirements for some weeks, if not months. Trees, shrubs, roses and perennials will benefit from a good-quality, slow-release granular feed scattered around the base in spring and autumn. Roses and shrubs also benefit from a liquid foliar feed whilst in full growth and flowering (follow the manufacturer's instructions).

Good old horse manure is a fantastic feed for shrubs and roses, but it must be well-rotted, otherwise it will 'burn' the plant. Used as a mulch at the base of the plant, as it decomposes it will release nutrients into the soil. Worm activity will also take nutrients deeper into the soil and improve its structure.

Seaweed-based feeds are very popular and freshly gathered seaweed used as a mulch is hugely beneficial. If it is freshly gathered, seaweed should be soaked in a bucket of water to remove some of the salt.

If a plant is looking very sad and unwell, first aid can be administered by giving a dose of liquid feed. Because it is quickly absorbed, it acts like a tonic, giving the plant a boost. Supported by a scattering of slow-release granular feed at the base, this should do the trick and the plant should start to look much better after a few days.

Weather Effects

When they are in growth, plants produce new shoots that are soft and tender. Exposure to weather, especially some of the extreme weather experienced in more recent years (particularly winds), can have a damaging effect on these vulnerable shoots.

Plant Choices by Type

The type of root system a plant has is a major consideration when selecting plants for a slope. The deep roots of plants such as trees and shrubs will help to stabilize the soil, contributing to a reduction in soil erosion and water loss. Trees not only add height, breadth and a wonderful skeletal structure in the winter, but also create shade, which prevents excess surface evaporation. Low-growing ground-cover plants

Table 6.1 Weather effects

WEATHER	IMPACT	WHAT TO LOOK OUT FOR
Sun	Too much hot sun can scorch young plants and dry out leaves and soil. Insufficient sun results in etiolated/straggly growth; loss of variegation on some variegated plants; reduced or no flowering; weakness in the plant, making it vulnerable to pests and disease.	Browning or drooping of leaves. In perennials the whole plant may collapse. Roots will be brittle and dry.
Wind	Strong, cold wind dries out foliage, especially tender new growth and newly planted specimens. Dries out soil and can cause soil erosion of fine soils.	Browning and curling of leaves, plant death. Lack of moisture can cause plants to droop.
Frost/ice/snow	Water frozen in the ground will deprive the plant of moisture. Weight of snow can bend/snap branches causing microscopic damage and creating an entry point for pests and diseases.	Frost-damaged new growth will be seen as blackened foliage and may be soft and mushy. Frost can damage early spring flowers such as camellias and magnolias, causing browning on the flowers and buds.

will also reduce surface erosion and evaporation and disguise unsightly areas at ground level, while requiring little maintenance.

The ideal planting scheme for a sloping site may be a combination of plants that are tolerant of wind and occasional drought and have wide-spreading root zones to anchor them to the slope. A selection of trees, shrubs, perennials and ground cover, despite being more difficult to establish, will also make a beautiful scheme for a sloping site. For a large sloping garden, the better the plants are suited to the given environment, the less maintenance they will require.

Fig. 6.5 Amphitheatre effect of planting on a slope.

Grass: Turf or Meadow?

Although expensive, turf grass is often a popular choice for the sloping garden due its instant ground-cover properties, but there are potential difficulties with both its establishment and its maintenance. These will generally be dependent on how steep or shallow the slope is. Simple maintenance tasks, such as mowing, on anything other than a reasonably shallow slope will present a challenge that may come to be dreaded over time. Add to that the fact that water will simply run off this high moisture-loving plant, pre-disposing it to drying out and possibly dying. Clearly, laying turf on a slope is not a decision to be taken lightly. Even a flat lawn with optimum water absorption will become brown and scorched in a hot, dry summer. The watering issue could be resolved by installing an irrigation system, but this can prove expensive if the water is metered and, no matter how sophisticated, it will not prevent water draining away down the slope.

Meadow turf is a modern-day alternative to turf grass, which may appeal to a garden owner looking for a more naturalistic and sustainable approach. It is a low-maintenance option, with minimal mowing requirements – just a couple of times a year – and is far less susceptible to the effects of drying out, as its mix includes tough grasses that form a thick root mat. The flower varieties are self-seeding and very drought-tolerant and, once established, all the plants in the mix will stabilize the soil. It is an all-round good planting solution for the sloping site. It not only looks picturesque in full flower but also provides a fantastic wildlife-friendly eco-habitat for insects, bees, butterflies, moths, hoverflies and small mammals. This option allows the gardener to sit back and relax in the knowledge that they are helping the environment, will have to undertake minimal maintenance, and will have a beautiful meadow slope to look at.

Fig. 6.6 *Cupressus sempervirens.*

Styles and Themes

Both the hard and soft landscaping of a garden will define its style. For example, an Italianate-style garden will be evocative of Italy and the Mediterranean by using classical sculpture, extravagant water features and terrazzo or terracotta tiles, all softened by and decorated with Mediterranean plants such as clipped topiary, slim, pencil-like Cupressus sempervirens and lots of brightly coloured geraniums.

There are several recognized garden styles to choose from, or you may want to develop a garden with a simple layout and a planting scheme chosen purely for personal reasons, such as favourite colours or shapes, or because the plants remind you of a loved one. The

BELOW: Fig. 6.7 A garden in the Mediterranean style.

most effective style or theme for a sloping garden, even though it is more costly, is one that includes terracing. The flat areas, or terraces, interlinked by steps for ease of access, will allow for relatively problem-free planting and successful establishment of the plants, and will reduce the physical demands of ongoing maintenance. In terms of style, terracing fits into the Mediterranean/formal amphitheatre spectrum. Generally speaking, there are ten identifiable garden styles:

- Mediterranean;
- Formal/Informal;
- Traditional;
- Cottage;
- Contemporary;
- Architectural;
- Chinese/Japanese;
- Scree/Gravel;
- Prairie/Naturalistic;
- Colour-schemed.

Plant Selection

The most successful planting schemes draw from all the plant groups to create balance, diversity of species and seasonal interest. The latter is important if a garden is to keep its owner and visitors in touch with the cycles of nature, as they observe the changes that take place through the year.

Generally, when putting together a planting scheme, you will be looking at choosing from the five main groups:

- trees;
- shrubs;
- perennials;
- bulbs; and
- annuals.

For more information on the plant groups, *see* Chapter 8.

Your plant selection will be influenced by a number of factors. One of these is of course visual preference. For a start, there may be certain colours that you absolutely want in the garden. This preference may be linked to their effect on the mind – for example, blues tend to have a relaxing effect, while reds are stimulating – although you may not be aware of this. Conversely, there may be certain colours you dislike, for various reasons. You may prefer plant shapes that are particularly striking and give a wow factor – for example, exciting or dramatic spiky architectural stems or leaf shapes – or you may like plants that are lower to the ground, creating soft mounds. Finally, you will certainly be influenced by your overall vision for the garden – are you aiming for a traditional or contemporary look and feel, or some other style?

It is useful to think about plants in terms of the effect they will have on the overall planting scheme. Foliage, form and flower colour are the three main factors to consider during this process (for more on this, *see* Chapter 8). Certain plants from the different groups may be selected in order to achieve particular effects. Trees and shrubs tend to give a very static feel due to their woody framework, but a scheme with both a strong structure and movement can be created by combining plants such as floaty grasses with some evergreens or trees and shrubs. Topiary, angular-shaped beds and lawns will give a formal effect, while loose drifts of planting and use of curves will give a softer, more dynamic informal effect.

While visual preferences are important, however, they should not be allowed to dominate your decision-making completely. You must still be sure to select plants according to their suitability for the site conditions and environment, as well as for their aesthetic appeal. The following factors should always be considered when choosing plants:

- The needs of the area: for example, a garden in the Cotswolds will have alkaline, chalky/limey soil that tends to be low in nutrients, limiting the number of plants that will thrive in it.
- Growth habit: a mixture of shapes – low-growing, medium and tall – provides more balance and is more interesting to look at.
- Season of interest: plants perform differently through the year. Some may be of interest in just one season, while others provide colour or striking structure in more than one season. Some flower in the spring; some do not flower at all, but offer colourful autumn foliage. When selecting plants, understanding their season of interest will help you to create a scheme that is appealing all year round.

The Process of Planning a Planting Scheme

Planning a planting scheme for the first time – particularly a scheme for a large sloping garden – can seem an intimidating and onerous task. What plants from the five main groups should you choose? How many will you need? Where can you buy them at a reasonable price?

To avoid feeling completely overwhelmed, and making expensive mistakes that you may regret in a couple of years' time, you might decide to use the services of a garden designer. They will prepare a scaled planting plan and a detailed costing, and will organize the supply of the plants, relieving you of all the angst and uncertainty. If you are not confident in your plant knowledge, this is probably advisable, whether you have a large or smaller sloping garden.

Table 6.2 Planting scheme procedure for the professional

ACTION	CONSIDERATIONS
Define soil type Moisture-retentive/free-draining? Acid or alkaline.	Specify soil prep required.
Define site conditions.	Aspect? Sunny or shady? Indicate these areas on plan. Prevailing wind? Dry or moisture-retentive soil?
Plants Define type/planting style required?	Draft plant list and select plants accordingly for all of the above. Ensure seasonal interest.
Clarify maintenance requirements	Low or higher maintenance? Select plants accordingly.
Draft scaled planting plan.	**Considerations:** Eventual height and width of plant at maturity (plants should fit the space in 7–10 years) Specific colour scheme required? Season of interest? Evergreen/deciduous, flower, foliage colour, berries, seed heads. Ensure good balance – select from each group (trees, shrubs, perennials, climbers, bulbs). Ensure balance of evergreens and deciduous so garden is not bare in winter. Right plant, right place.
Management See plant schedule table. Prepare plant schedule with quantities and pot sizes. Calculate plant numbers.	Email to nurseries for costing. Plants will be ordered from nurseries for value and availability of varying pot sizes.
Organize plant supply.	Delivery date – be on site for delivery to inspect plants and sign them off.
Organize labour.	
Establishment	Make follow up visits to ensure plants are establishing well. Identify any problems and advise accordingly.

Table 6.3 Example of a plant schedule

PLANT SCHEDULE FOR [NAME OF PROJECT]					
QTY	POT	PLANT	QTY	POT	PLANT
		CONIFERS		**1-3L**	**HERBACEOUS**
1	15L	*Thuja occidentalis* 'Danica'	2		*Achillea* 'Terrracotta'
2	3L	*Thuja occidentalis* 'Smaragd'	2		*Achillea* 'Lilac Beauty'
2	3L	*Thuja occidentalis* 'Tiny Tim'	2		*Ajuga* 'Chocolate Chip'
			3		*Astrantia major*
	2/3L	**SHRUBS**	1		*Echinacea purpurea*
1		*Leycesteria formosa*	3		*Euphorbia carach.* 'Martinii'
2		*Phormium* 'Tri-color'	3		*Geranium macrorrhizum* 'Spessart'
1		*Photinia fraserii* 'Red Robin'	2		*Geranium* 'Blue Cloud'
2		*Pittosporum* 'Tom Thumb'	2		*Geranium* 'Vision Violet'
1		*Physocarpus* 'Diablo'	2		*Geranium* 'Patricia'
1		*Sambucus nigra* 'Black Lace'	3		*Geranium* 'Anne Folkard'
1		*Phlomis tub.* 'Bronze Flamingo'	1		*Geranium* 'Brookside'
			3		*Geranium phaeum* 'Samobar'
	2/3L	**GRASSES**	2		*Gaura lindheimeri*
1		*Calamagrostis acut.* 'Karl Foester'	1		*Helenium* 'Moerheim Beauty'
1		*Eragrostis curvula*	1		*Helenium* 'Sahin's Early Flowerer'
1		*Miscanthus sacchariflorus*	2		*Hemerocallis* 'Stella D'or'
1		*Molinia caer ssp. arund.* 'Karl Foerster'	3		*Heuchera* 'Ruby Bells'
2		*Stipa tenuissima*	6		*Heuchera* 'Palace Purple'
			2		*Nepeta* 'Dawn til Dusk'
	2/3L	**FERNS**	2		*Nepeta* 'Six Hills Giant'
5		*Polystichum setiferum*	2		*Penstemon* 'Husker Red'
			1		*Penstemon* 'Mixed Pinks'
		HERBS	3		*Tellima grandiflora*
1		*Origanum vulgare* 'Aurea'	2		*Rudbeckia* 'Deamii'
1		*Salvia officinalis* 'Purpurescens'	3		*Salvia* 'Blue Queen'
2		*Rosmarinus prostrata*	2		*Sedum matron* 'Purpurea'
[Contact details for the sender can go in this box]					

Following a structured procedure when planning a planting scheme will help to smooth the journey from bare soil to planted soil to a lovely established garden.

If you feel you lack the knowledge base to undertake the planning yourself, you should engage a garden designer. You can expect them to undertake the following tasks:

1. Draft a scaled design/layout plan.
2. Provide an accurate calculation of plant numbers.
3. Provide an accurate costing of plants.
4. Provide an accurate costing of labour.
5. Provide an accurate costing of materials such as membrane, tree bark and turf, if required.
6. Recommend contractors.
7. Oversee the planting.

The procedures followed by a professional garden designer are covered in Table 6.2.

If you decide to undertake the planning of the planting scheme yourself, you will need to be on top of the following tasks:

1. Identify soil type: specify prep required.
2. Plants: organize supply of plants and labour if required.
3. Management: be on site to supervise the planting.
4. Establishment: follow up and advice to ensure successful establishment of the plants.

The Plant Schedule

The plant schedule is more than just a list. It is a document that organizes all the plants required for the project into certain categories – conifers, shrubs, herbs, and so on – and specifies the names of all the plants, and the quantity and pot sizes required. The table format makes it easy to see at a glance the varieties and numbers involved, and enables the nursery or other supplier to pull out the plants quickly if a planting plan is being prepared. The schedule will be printed on to the plan for on-site use, and can be emailed to suppliers for costings.

If it is a large garden that is to be planted, the schedule can be further organized into specific areas, for example, patio borders, lawn borders, and so on. When several people are working on the planting, this will enable them to know which plants to put where. When the plants arrive on site they can be checked off against the schedule and organized straightaway into their area groups, to save time and energy. All in all, a detailed plant schedule facilitates the organization and execution of the planting project and helps it to run smoothly.

Maintenance

Following the planting, consideration should be given to the basic care and ongoing maintenance of the plants. Once there has been a reasonable amount of growth and the plants are better established, a less intensive care regime is needed and a more long-term management strategy can be commenced. This should incorporate four main maintenance tasks:

- Watering: requirements will depend on the soil type and the specific plants selected. How are the plants going to be watered and how often will they need watering? Is an irrigation system required? Installation for this will need to be scheduled.
- Feeding: again, requirements will depend on the condition of the soil and its type, and on the plants selected. Has plenty of good topsoil, soil conditioner and compost been added to the soil in the soil prep? How often does the soil type require feeding? Remember, free-draining soil in particular needs regular feeding. Do some of the plants selected need more feed than others? For example, roses and flowering shrubs can be hungry plants.
- Mowing and other lawn maintenance tasks: how often will the grass need mowing? The type of grass, either formal or meadow, will influence what needs to be done and when.
- Pruning: identify any trees or shrubs that have specific pruning requirements. Pruning is carried out to shape plants, to encourage flowering or simply to manage their size. Not all shrubs can be pruned at the same time, for example, a spring-flowering shrub should not be pruned until after it has flowered.

It always helps to have a document that lists the relevant tasks, along with the time of year when they should

Table 6.4 Example of a maintenance schedule

MAINTENANCE SCHEDULE												
TASK	Jan	Feb	Mar	April	May	June	July	Aug	Sept	Oct	Nov	Dec
Tree pruning												
Shrub pruning												
Mulch												
Watering												
Feeding												
Splitting perennials												
Mowing: meadow												
Mowing: formal lawn												
Bulb planting												

be carried out, and how often. A maintenance schedule (*see* Table 6.4) can be quickly drawn up on a PC, saved and printed out, to be kept somewhere to hand for easy reference. A schedule like this will be particularly useful when looking after a large garden.

Budget for Planting

The way the planting budget is managed will depend very much upon the size of the sloping garden, the finances available, and the extent of the planting to be done. Generally, of course, the bigger the garden the more costly the planting will be, but there are variables and options that can be employed to ease the financial impact:

- Sections: planting can be divided into separate sections or areas, each to be tackled at a designated time, therefore spreading the cost over a timescale of your choosing.
- Nursery supplier: plants bought from a nursery supplier will usually cost less than those from a garden centre.
- Pot size: plants in smaller pot sizes will cost less. The sizes on offer are usually 9cm, 1L, 2L and 3L.

Fig. 6.8 Plant pot sizes.

Fig. 6.9 A bare-root shrub.

Fig. 6.10 A bare-root perennial..

A plant in a 9cm pot will be the smallest, probably a first-year split or cutting, but as long as it has a good root ball it should establish very well. It may even suffer less transplant shock than a bigger plant.

- Size: some plants can be selected at semi-mature size, but it is advisable to plant some larger trees and shrubs to provide structure for instant effect.
- Seed: some elements, such as areas of grass, could be grown from seed.
- Bare root: trees, shrubs, roses, hedging and perennials can all be purchased as bare roots. This is a very cost-effective way of acquiring plants, as it involves no additional labour costs, such as potting into compost and administering after care. The plants arrive as bare roots wrapped in damp hessian or plastic with no soil. They have a specific availability season, which runs from November to February or March, when they are dormant. It is important to follow the supplier's planting instructions – for example, to soak bare-root hedging, roses and shrubs for at least 24 hours prior to planting, to ensure that the roots are damp when they go into the ground or pot.

Clearly, whether a garden is large or small, flat or sloping, it is very important to plan the planting scheme carefully, giving consideration to soil conditions, aspect, visual preferences and budget, and following the procedures in the logical order. The ultimate aim is a beautiful planting scheme that will only get better with time. This is achieved by carrying out appropriate soil prep to maximize the plants' chances of survival, getting the plants in the ground at an acceptable cost to the owner, and establishing a reasonable schedule of maintenance for the long term.

CHAPTER 7

PLANTING DESIGN THEORY

What is Planting Design?

The subject of planting design is a huge one, which encourages the designer and the observer to consider plants in their entirety, not just as an entity that needs some soil and some sun. It has its own rules and principles and encompasses many different styles and concepts.

A garden is usually a selection of plants, lawn and some form of hard landscaping. All over the world there are many different types of garden, all with their own individual planting and landscaping schemes. Regardless of the scheme or style being adopted, achieving a successful planting arrangement requires precise and considered planning, otherwise known as 'planting design'. Among other things, it involves the selection of plants for a variety of reasons, not least the particular growing conditions and the specific needs of the garden being developed. Some owners may be looking for a garden that requires minimal maintenance, to allow them simply to relax and enjoy time in the space with friends and family, without having to spend precious hours mowing, weeding and digging. Today, a garden also increasingly fulfils an extended role in accommodating a home office or home gym, or acting as a place for 'green therapy'. When faced with such a tick list of additional needs, getting it right will demand thought and a structured approach; the top priority is that the garden should be a pleasure rather than a worry.

Fig. 7.1 Waterfall and ferns.

Of course, all plants require some level of maintenance, varying from high to low, but surely a garden without plants would seem to be lacking in life and energy. There is so much enjoyment to be found in the simple pleasures associated with plants – the sight of the beautiful colours of flowers, and of graceful grasses swaying in the breeze, the memories evoked by gorgeous smells, the taste of herbs picked for cooking, and the sound of birdsong and buzzing bees, and the rustling of fallen leaves in autumn. It is these qualities that are at the core of todays 'garden prescriptions', which recommend time spent in a garden for the therapy and management of stress-related issues and mental health problems. These are the experiences that a designer should seek to create in a garden and choosing plants with this in mind is a major component of planting design.

If a sloping garden is to succeed, it is vital to spend time beforehand on planting design. That may involve sketching and scribbling in a handbook, or putting something together in a computer design programme. It will certainly involve researching 'right plant, right place' and compiling plant lists. All these activities will contribute to the success of all aspects of the scheme. Visiting a garden centre without a plan can be exciting, but at worst it can be bewildering. Allowing yourself to be lured by fantastic displays of brightly coloured flowers, cleverly grouped together to maximize their impact and to tempt the customer, is bound to end in disappointment. Buying just one plant on a whim because of how it looks at the garden centre, without thought of how it will perform in the planting scheme at home, is very rarely a successful strategy. To avoid wasting money on purchasing plants that will not thrive or simply do not look right, make sure you have a list of plants that is specific to your site. It will help you resist the temptation to buy just because you have been drawn in by an attractive display. Taking time early on to ensure that the overall scheme will work in terms of seasonal interest, colour and variety of shapes will pay huge dividends in the long run.

Plant Characteristics

Most people who are interested in horticulture and design initially think of a plant purely from the perspective of its horticultural needs. What soil does it like? Does it prefer full sun or shade? While such practical horticultural considerations are usually the ones that come to mind first, and also form the framework within which planting schemes are appraised, the process of designing a successful planting scheme is rather more complex than the simple fulfilment of the plants' growing requirements. It also involves close observation of individual plants and a recognition of plant characteristics. Such characteristics are not often defined, but they are easily seen when you become familiar with them. For example, you might want to identify the outline shape of a plant, such as 'globe' or 'cone', and contrast it with, say, the softer mound shape of a small shrub.

Once the principles of planting design have been understood and taken on board, a eureka moment occurs. A door is opened to a world of perceiving and

Fig. 7.2 The spiky, architectural shape of *Cordyline australis*.

Fig. 7.3 Nine plant shapes.

Planting Design as an Art Form

So, what it is about a successful planting scheme that makes it work? Like art, the observer's appreciation of planting design is a very subjective matter. What is beautiful for one designer/gardener/garden owner may not be attractive to another. Take the work of gardener and garden writer Christopher Lloyd (2 March 1921–27 January 2006) as an example. Lloyd's life was spent gardening and writing about plants and, along with his head gardener and great friend Fergus Garrett, he developed the wonderful, world-renowned garden at Great Dixter, near Rye in East Sussex. He was a talented plantaholic, but his work was sometimes controversial. He loved to experiment with his plantings and with the use of colour, and his schemes often caused surprise in plant lovers and visitors to Great Dixter. His striking, high-impact colour combinations, such as the vibrant mauve of Erysium 'Bowles Mauve' next to bright orange Geum, were quite unconventional at the time, but they certainly worked! Lloyd is now considered to have had a significant influence on the art of garden design, and his death in 2006 was a great loss to the world of horticulture.

Fig. 7.4 *Erysium* 'Bowles Mauve' planted up with orange tulips.

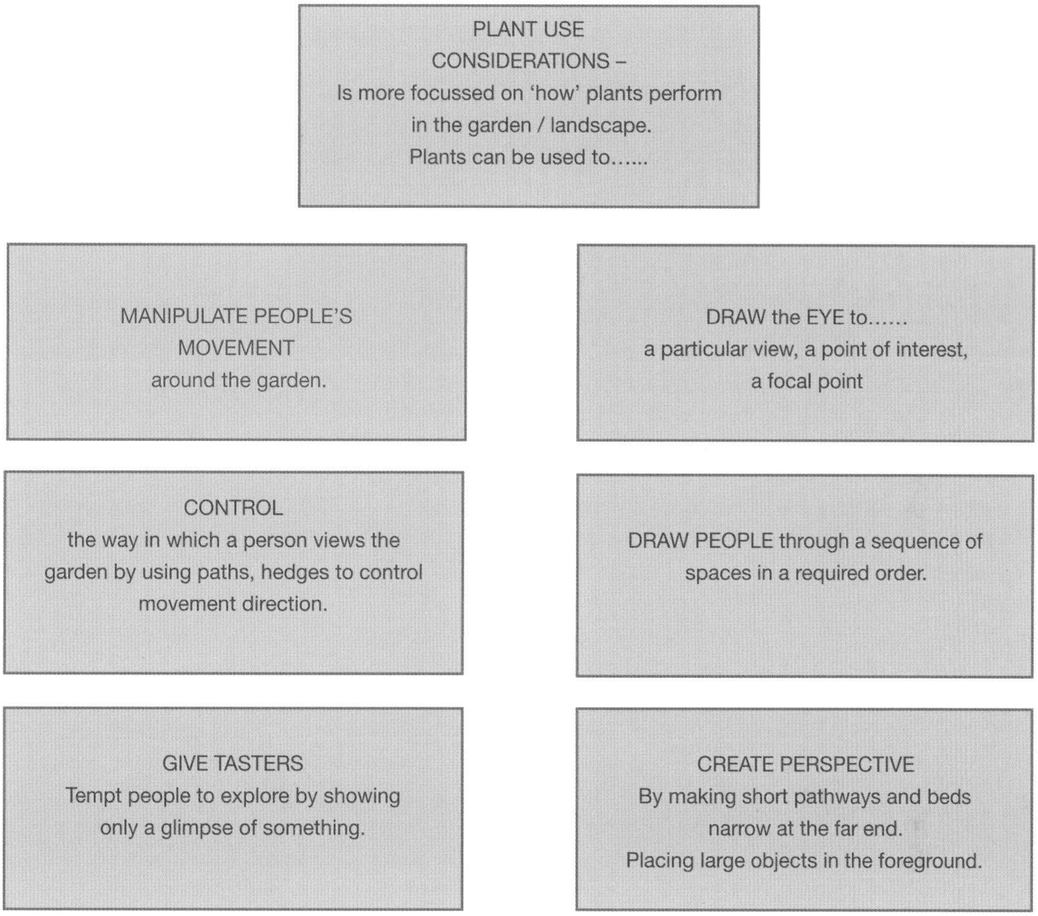

Fig. 7.5 Plant use considerations.

observing plants through completely new eyes. Plants are so much more than just their growing requirements; they have characteristics and personalities of their own, which they bring to the garden. For example, *Cordyline australis* may be defined as a Mediterranean plant that likes free-draining soil and plenty of sun. That describes the growing requirements of the Cordyline, but if you look more closely and describe the plant's individual characteristics, you might add that it is bright green in colour, that it has a spiky, dramatic, modern-looking architectural shape and that it looks rather like a firework exploding. These are the qualities and characteristics that the Cordyline will bring to the planting scheme; as an added bonus, it is evergreen, so will provide interest in all the seasons.

One of the fundamental skills of planting design is an ability to look at, observe and describe how the plant appears to you. One major characteristic is the outline shape; there are approximately nine basic versions of this (*see* Fig. 7.3). Once the designer or gardener has started to observe plants in this way, they really get to know them from a completely different perspective.

Plant Use

The huge variations between what two different people may like make it difficult to identify the components of a successful planting scheme. Where do you start? Do you aim for a standard of horticultural 'perfection', with a collection of perfectly formed, unblemished plants and perfectly clipped dwarf hedging, or do you go for a scheme in which the plants are used for their striking shapes, foliage or flower colour? Everyone will have a personal reaction to the planting style or selection of plants.

In order to achieve a successful planting scheme, a designer needs a structure or framework of guidelines within which to work. The choice of plants will partly be governed by a client brief, which may include instructions such as 'lots of colour', 'low maintenance', and so on. This brief should be combined with the 'plant use considerations', which focus on how plants perform in the garden or landscape, and how they may be used for specific purposes.

Choosing plants for a planting scheme is not simply a question of deciding which colours you prefer. Instead, you need to take a broader view and think about the planting from several different perspectives, including shape, season of interest, performance – and colour. This will enable you to create a scheme that is interesting for more than just a few weeks in the summer. As each season unfolds, a different type of plant beauty will be revealed, through the flowers, foliage colour, berries, evergreen shapes, seed heads, and so much more.

Following the planting design principles (*see* below) will help you make plant selections for specific reasons, enable a more structured approach and increase awareness of how plants can look very different when planted on a slope as opposed to a flat piece of ground. It will also help you make use of each plant's very individual qualities and effects.

Planting Design Principles

The criteria governing the planning and assessment of a planting scheme are known as the planting design principles. These are the foundations upon which planting design rests. Thousands of years ago, the first three design principles were defined by Roman writer, architect and engineer Marcus Vitruvius Pollio (born c.80–70 BC, died after c.15 BC). Over time, in order to keep pace with changing tastes in planting styles and other developments, the number of design principles has increased from three to eight. Of course, opinions vary as to what these principles should be, however, working within a framework at least provides everyone with a common language with which to assess, observe and plan planting schemes. Regardless of whether the scheme is small or large, understanding and knowing these principles will clearly help with planting design work.

The eight commonly recognized planting design principles are:

- form;
- rhythm;
- focal point;
- harmony;
- contrast;
- texture;
- balance; and
- unity.

Form

The overall shape of a plant is referred to as its 'form'. It is what you see when you look at its outline. Evergreen plants provide permanent form throughout the year. Excellent examples of evergreens, with very distinctive forms, can be found in the conifer family, such as the distinct round or globe shape of *Thuja occidentalis* 'Danica' (*see* Fig. 7.6). It is to this plant group that designers often turn for long-term seasonal interest and a fantastic choice of distinctive shapes. There are of course other options, such as box (Buxus), although in recent years there has been a particular issue with the box blight fungus. Form can also be introduced into a planting scheme by using clipped evergreens (topiary), commonly yew (Taxus) shaped into balls and spirals, and standard bay trees.

Through the winter months, certain deciduous trees and shrubs provide a very distinctive skeletal type of 'form' with their outline shape and branch formation. The hornbeam *Carpinus betulus* 'Fastigiata' (*see* Fig. 7.7) is a classic example, which is easily recognizable even when its branches are bare.

Clearly, the design principle of form is an important one. Evergreens, particularly, contribute to a strong structure in a garden and at the same time can provide focal points to any planting scheme. One example is dwarf evergreen hedging, which can be used to guide the eye and direct movement, as well as to distract attention from something less attractive.

Fig. 7.6 *Thuja occidentalis* 'Danica'.

Fig. 7.7 Pyramidal hornbeam (*Carpinus betulus* 'Fastigiata').

Fig. 7.8 Clipped yew balls.

Fig. 7.9 Standard bay tree.

Rhythm

Rhythm in the garden can be achieved by considering the spacing in between plants. Typically, a plant type is repeated, and the eye singles out and follows the repeated shape or colour. An avenue or line of trees is usually defined by low-level planting – and sometimes no planting at all – below the tree line, so that the tree trunks are exposed. The trunks seen at specific intervals create the rhythm. Rhythm can also be created by repeating a certain colour at regular intervals within the scheme.

The rate of the rhythm is created by the speed at which the eye moves from plant to plant or tree to tree. The smaller the space in between the plants, the faster the rhythm, and the further the plants are apart, the slower the rhythm, so spacing can be used to either slow down or speed up the observer's journey. It can also direct the eye to a specific point such as a sculpture, focal point plant or maybe a bench with a view that the owner wishes the visitor to see.

Fig. 7.10 Trees planted with long gaps in between, to create a slow rhythm.

Focal Point

A focal point is created in a garden by the specific positioning of a plant or object, in such a way that it acts as a point of interest. In a planting scheme or border, a focal point can be achieved by choosing a plant that either has an unusual growth habit and strong form, such as *Viburnum plicatum* 'Lanarth', or displays beautiful foliage colour, such as *Acer palmatum dissectum* 'Atropurpureum'. Frequently seen as a focal point plant in the spring are Magnolia trees, which flower at a time when there is very little else in flower to compete with them.

Fig. 7.11 A row of evergreens planted close together, creating a fast rhythm.

In the autumn, focal point plants are more likely to be trees that display stunning seasonal colour, such as the Liquidambar or sweet gum, with its deep red leaves, or the field maples, with their bright yellows and oranges.

A focal point can be created at the end of a vista in the direct eyeline of the viewer by the strategic positioning of a plant or group of plants in an ornate pot that is raised up from the ground. Structures such as pergolas, arbours, summerhouses can also be used as focal points.

Fig. 7.12 Horizontal growth habit of *Viburnum plicatum* 'Lanarth'.

Fig. 7.13 *Acer palmatum* 'Dissectum atropurpureum'.

Fig. 7.15 Autumn foliage colour of Liquidambar.

Fig. 7.14 *Magnolia stellata*.

Fig. 7.16 Yellow autumn foliage colour.

Fig. 7.17 Pergola used as a focal point.

Fig. 7.18 Summerhouse used as a focal point.

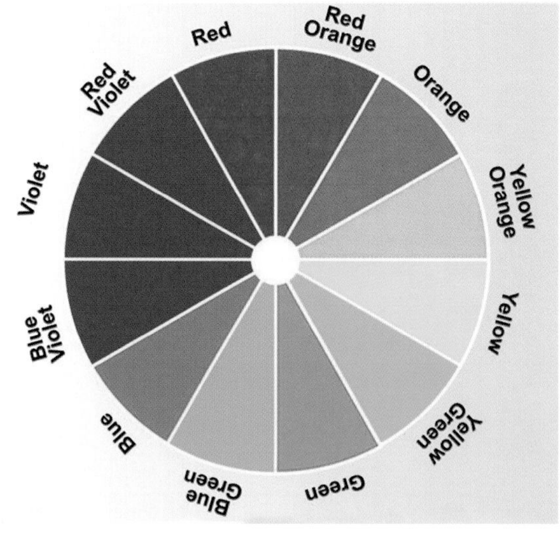

Fig. 7.19 The colour wheel.

Table 7.1 Colour, harmony and contrast

COLOUR EFFECTS AND HOW TO USE THEM		
COLOUR	EFFECT	SLOPING GARDEN
Red-based colours (red, orange)	Advances to the eye	Do not use at top of slope as it will make it appear closer.
		If slope is away from house – downhill – use red on far boundary to make it appear closer.
		A long narrow garden/slope can be foreshortened by planting red flowers on the rear boundary.
	Appears hot/ warm	Using red will create a stimulating, energizing effect on the viewer.
		If slope is south-facing, it will feel hotter if red flowers are planted.
Red-based purples	Appear warm	Add drama and could be used on south-facing slope.
		Use at top of slope to make it seem further away.
Blue-based colours (blue, lilacs, pale blue	Recede away from the eye.	If short slope away from house, use blues to make it seem further away.
		A short/wide garden/slope can be made to feel longer and wider by planting blue on the boundaries.
	Appear cool, some appear cold.	Using blues will create a cool, calming effect on the viewer.
		A north-facing slope will feel cooler if blue flowers are planted.

Harmony

A harmonized planting scheme will be pleasing to all who see it, with a dominant tone and colour in various shades that run through all the plants and are close to each other on the colour wheel (*see* Fig. 7.19). This gives all the plants something in common – a link that creates visual harmony. Choosing colours from the same range – for example, blues that harmonize with lilacs, yellows that harmonize with oranges – ensures that the planting is aesthetically pleasing. For example, the soft colours of pale blue clematis and Perovskia work well against the green and cream variegated foliage of *Phalaris arundinacea var. picta*.

Fig. 7.20 Harmonizing colours.

The way that colour is used in a garden creates a response in the observer, and harmonizing colours are easy on the eye, and relaxing and calming to look at, thus creating a tranquil effect.

Harmony can also be achieved by using plant shapes that blend together and support each other, thus bringing out the best qualities of all the plants.

Contrast

Contrast is another important design principle in the garden and is created by using colours from opposite sides of the colour wheel (*see* Fig. 7.19). Contrasting colours are striking to look at, they grab the visual attention and tend to dominate in a planting scheme, as is the case with the bright yellow of Carex elata 'Aurea' against the dark maroon of Euphorbia 'Chameleon' (*see* Fig. 7.21).

Planting combinations that will command attention include red or purple with yellow, and lime green or bright pink with orange. The effect of such combinations will be energizing and stimulating.

Fig. 7.21 Contrasting colours.

Texture

Plant foliage is the most significant provider of texture in a garden. One classic example is Stachys byzantina, otherwise known as 'Lamb's Ears' because of its large, soft, grey furry leaves. In contrast, you might consider the large, smooth, green, glossy reflective surface of a hosta leaf (*see* Fig. 7.23). The strongest quality of smooth, glossy leaves is that they reflect light and bounce it around. Over the years, many varieties of hosta have been bred with variegation in their leaves, varying from very bright whites to creamy yellows with green or green blue as the dominant leaf colour. This is why the hosta is a very popular plant choice for use in shade; it does not merely tolerate low light levels, but even thrives in them, and increases or at least gives the impression of increasing light levels in shady areas.

Fig. 7.22 *Stachys byzantina* 'Lamb's Ears'.

Fig. 7.23 Hosta leaf.

Fig. 7.24 *Spiky Eryngium zabelii* 'Big Blue'.

Other specific plant textures are offered by the spiky Eryngium family, the coarse, hairy leaves of Brunnera macrophylla 'Jack Frost', the very smooth shiny leaves of Choysia and Laurel, and there are many more. Overall, the effect of using texture in a garden is to create both visual and tactile interest for the viewer. For the plant itself, its texture is a clever survival mechanism. For example, the soft, furry surface of a stachys leaf protects it from scorching in hot sun, while the smooth shiny surface of a hosta leaf directs rainwater down the stem and off the leaf to the base of the plant, as well as reflecting light.

Balance

Balance is a design principle that needs to be achieved in the garden, not only between planting and structures such as the property, but also between the plants themselves. A balance can be struck by considering the plants' dimensions – height and width – along with their shapes. As a general rule of thumb, taller plants are placed at the rear of the border and plant heights are decreased towards the front of the border, creating balance between the different heights. However, this rule can be modified and taller 'see-through' plants may be placed nearer the front of the border; because of their structure, their height will not dominate and they will not block the view of smaller plants behind.

The garden designer needs to be aware of a lack of balance, too. For example, if part of a mature hedge dies, leaving a gap, the gap may be replanted with a younger plant, but the hedge will always look out of balance in this area, as the new planting will be smaller than the existing hedge.

Fig. 7.25 *Brunnera macrophylla* 'Jack Frost'.

Fig. 7.26 A nicely balanced planting scheme, achieved by reducing plant heights from each side down to the lavender-flanked pathway in the centre.

Fig. 7.27 A balanced planting scheme, with the added impact of using some very strong plant shapes.

By not using too much of any one colour the planting designer is also seeking to achieve a balance between colours. If there is too much use of strong colours such as red, orange and bright yellow, those plants will dominate the entire scheme. When using strong colours, less is definitely more! Red is a very dominant colour that 'advances' towards the eye; used conservatively, it can work to highlight certain points in the planting, but if overused it dominates and the effect of the rest of the planting becomes diluted. However, many public gardens will feature one 'hot' border, where red is used with other strong colours such as yellow and orange from the same part of the colour wheel. This can be really effective and striking.

The aim should be to achieve a balance of planting interest throughout the seasons. It is not desirable to have an interesting summer garden that becomes bare and uninteresting through the winter months. This is where the use of evergreens, and plants with strong shapes or form alongside plants with autumn foliage colour and/or berries comes into its own, to create a scheme that has appeal all through the year. In winter, gardens tend to be green, beige/grey and brown, without any of the bright colours that come with summer, so shape and form become more important.

Unity

Unity is a broad term that refers to the achievement of a planting scheme that appears as whole – a cohesive unit where every single plant plays its part, and none is particularly dominant over any other. It is like an orchestra in which all the sections come together to sound as one. That is not to say that a variety of colours and/or plant shapes cannot be used; when they are chosen with care, the overall effect can still be one of unity.

It is interesting to note that unity is a combination of all the planting design principles brought together in balance. If one principle is removed, the result is a planting scheme that seems to be missing something. It can be quite intangible – sometimes you look at a border or bed and say, 'Well, I like it, but....' It is not always possible to define exactly what it is that the scheme is lacking, but the observer instinctively knows that it is just not quite right. If a designer looks to the design principles and applies them, it is highly likely that the missing component will be recognized.

Planting Styles

What is the meaning of the term 'style' when applied to planting design? The usual examples that spring to mind when talking about style come from the world of fashion: for example, hippie style is identifiable by its characteristic long hair, tie-dye clothing, headbands, and strings of beads, while the Mod style is reflected in a smart, fitted clothing, such as a suit worn with a button-down collared shirt and tie, and short cut hair. These styles are in striking contrast with each other, and each is distinguished by distinctive characteristics that create a strong visual image. The world of planting style is no different. Each garden style is defined by a collection of differing elements, both in hard and soft landscaping, which when brought together are representative of a particular era in history or a plant community that is unique to a specific area, such as the Prairies of North America. When planning a planting scheme in a particular style, it is important to ask questions to ensure that the style will work and sit comfortably with its surrounding environment (*see* Fig. 7.28).

Influences

Gardens have evolved throughout history as a direct result of the social and cultural issues of the day. The growing of vegetables is one example. Dramatic change began in the eighteenth and nineteenth centuries, with the Enclosure Acts, which redefined land-

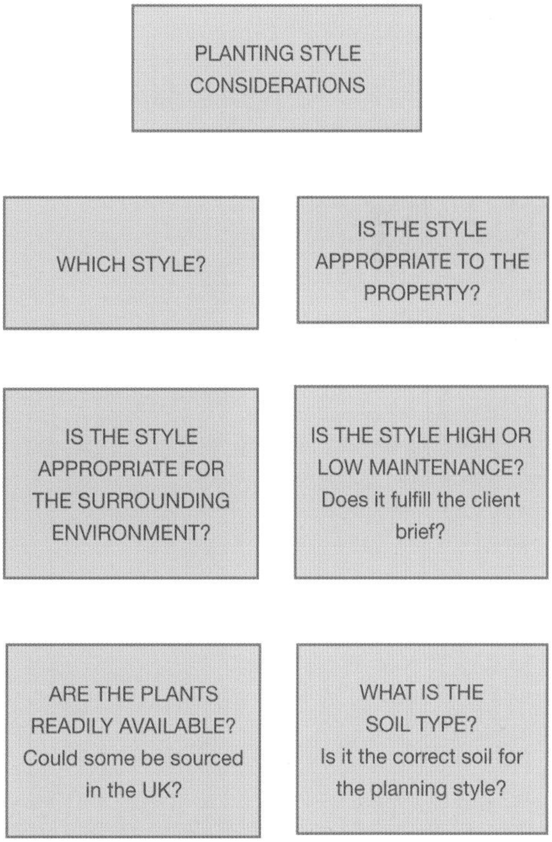

Fig. 7.28 Planting style considerations.

owner boundaries around the country. This was followed by great unrest amongst the peasants, who no longer had access to the land they had lived on and had cultivated in order to eke out an existence. The resultant rebellions gave rise to the Allotments Acts of the late nineteenth and twentieth centuries, which compensated the 'labouring poor' for the loss of their grazing rights with the opportunity to use a piece of land on which to grow food. An equally important historic change came about with the 'Dig for Victory' campaign of the Second World War. All of these societal and cultural events had a direct impact upon land and garden use, culminating in the further development of allotments for public use and of Victorian kitchen gardens. With these, the growing of vegetables for domestic use, rather than commercial, became the norm. Interestingly, both allotments and Victorian kitchen gardens have a very distinctive style, which immediately brings to mind a particular visual image.

Other garden styles seen in Britain have been influenced by various significant European architectural and historic movements, such as Romanesque, French and Italian Renaissance and Mediterranean.

Style and Aspect

A garden style is achieved by combining hard landscaping materials and soft landscaping (plants). However, the sense of the chosen style will not be achieved by simply combining these two elements in any area of the garden. There are other more subtle, but none the less essential, 'ingredients' that need to be in the mix. One of the most important of these is aspect – in other words, the direction in which the garden or border faces. As a general rule of thumb, the more a border faces south, the more sun it will receive, so a south-facing border will appear light, bright and 'sunny'.

With certain planting styles, the correct marriage of aspect and style is central to success. Is the style immediately recognizable? For example, a north-facing border planted in Mediterranean style would not succeed, for two reasons. First, from the perspective of horticultural needs, Mediterranean-type plants require full sun, so they would certainly not thrive – indeed, they might not even survive – in the cold shade of a north-facing border. Second, from a visual and psychological perspective, the onlooker recognizes and connects the plants with being sun-loving and will then question their position in the shade. It just will not look right.

The Nine Planting Styles

Generally speaking, there are nine planting/garden styles, which all make use of certain elements – in the hard landscaping and the plants – that work together to evoke each one:

Fig. 7.29 Mediterranean planting style.

Table 7.2 Mediterranean planting style.

CHARACTERISTICS	KEY PLANTS
Sunshine and good light. Strong colours. Architectural plants. Climbing plants. Scented plants. Use of pots, terracotta tiles. White walls.	*Cordyline australis.* Agapanthus. Geraniums and pelargoniums. Succulents. Citrus. Olive trees (*Olea europeus).* *Cupressus sempevirens* (can brown if exposed to too much wind).
	Herbs: Highly aromatic. Thyme, Rosemary, Marjoram, Bay (*Laurus nobilis*).
	Climbers: *Bougainvillea* 'Purple King' (in a South-facing, sheltered spot; will need over winter protection). Jasmine. Campsis (a climber with vibrant trumpet-shaped flowers).
	Hardy palms: *Trachycarpus fortunei.*

- Mediterranean;
- Formal/Informal;
- Cottage;
- Traditional;
- Contemporary;
- Architectural;
- Chinese/Japanese;
- Scree or Gravel garden;
- Prairie;
- Colour-schemed.

Mediterranean

Mediterranean garden style has a very relaxed, informal feel to it and lends itself perfectly to the lifestyle of al fresco eating. It is great for a sunny area in the garden for lazy lunches and barbecue evenings.

Formal and Informal

The formal style is predominantly governed by strong forms, whether in the hard or soft landscaping, and tends to be most suitable for properties with a formal house style such as Victorian and Georgian. Informal style is more relaxed, with random patterns, curving lines and use of 'softer' materials and plants.

Fig. 7.30 Formal planting style.

Table 7.3 Formal planting style.

CHARACTERISTICS	KEY PLANTS
Hard landscaping layout, often straight lines. Vistas. Statuary. Topiary. Pattern in hard landscaping or planting – knot garden.	Strong form, usually evergreen – conifers. Clipped topiary and hedging – Buxus, Euonymus, Escallonia. Often clipped dwarf hedging to edge the borders. Roses. Often linear, square-shaped beds and borders. Traditional planting mix – shrubs at back and perennial herbaceous plants towards the front. Traditional bedding plant schemes in summer (echoes of Victoriana).

Fig. 7.31 Informal planting style.

Table 7.4 Informal planting style.

CHARACTERISTICS	KEY PLANTS
Often long, sinuous curves for lawns, borders and hard landscape elements.	Very relaxed planting of loose drifts of mixed colour, soft, pastel colours that are easy on the eye.
Random slabbing pattern rather than square or rectangular slabs laid in a grid pattern.	Use of ornamental grasses to add movement: Miscanthus, Stipa, Pennisetum, Molinia.
Use of timber rather than brick and block.	A mix of traditional plants from the main groups of shrubs. Herbaceous perennials: Penstemon, Rudbeckia, Helenium, Malva, Echinacea.
	Bulbs in combination with roses, climbers, conifers. Roses and climbers planted on an obelisk or scrambling over an archway give a strong impression of a traditional garden. Heathers may be included, but only if the soil is acidic.

Cottage

Cottage garden planting style is very eclectic and plants from all groups can be used, sometimes alongside vegetables dotted through the beds. Remember that if a traditional cottage-style scheme has a high number of perennials, which will die down in the autumn, the garden can look quite bare in the winter months.

Fuchsias and pelargoniums may be used in containers, but those that are not hardy will need frost-free shelter in the winter.

Fiug. 7.32 Cottage planting style.

Table 7.5 Cottage planting style.

CHARACTERISTICS	KEY PLANTS
Loose, informal planting. Mixed colours, randomly distributed throughout. High maintenance, due to number of herbaceous perennials used. Spring and summer are main seasons of interest. Planted containers dotted around. Mix of flowers, vegetables and herbs.	Mixed field hedging for boundaries. Spring bulbs. Lavender (Old English style). Roses: such as Paul's Himalayan Musk (1848), vigorous and graceful with dainty, scented flowers, or the Noisette rose 'Gloire de Dijon' (1853).
Herbaceous perennials.	Leucanthemum, Hollyhocks, Sunflowers, Delphiniums, Dianthus (old-fashioned, scented varieties). Madonna Lilies, Sweet WilliamS, *Alchemilla mollis*, foxgloves (Digitalis).
Climbers, to scramble up a wall, porch over arches.	Honeysuckle (Lonicera). *Jasmine officinalis.* Clematis.
Roses.	e.g. Pauls Himalayan Musk (1848) – vigorous and graceful with dainty, scented flowers. or the Noisette rose 'Gloire de Dijon'(1853).
Herbs.	*Rosmarinus officinalis* (Rosemary), Salvia officinalis (sage), Thymes.
Bulbs.	Tulips, Narcissus, bluebells, Muscari.

Contemporary

The well-known, widely travelled John Brookes MBE is recognized as having been at the forefront of contemporary garden design in the UK. His influence is strikingly obvious in his gardens, where the use of hard landscaping is beautiful, showing the chosen material to the best of its potential. In addition, the connection between hard landscaping and the surrounding environment is seamless.

The planting in a contemporary-style garden is often conspicuous by its absence. In other words, there is very little of it. Sometimes, a specific plant group may be selected, such as Sedum, and only that plant group is used, or only one variety of plant is used.

Fig. 7.33 Contemporary planting style.

Table 7.6 Contemporary planting style.

CHARACTERISTICS	KEY PLANTS
Less is more - the dominant element of a Contemporary Garden is the hard landscaping, rather than the planting. Strong use of foliage shape – architectural. Colour contrasts. Use of several focal point plants, rather than one or two.	Sedums. Tree ferns. *Ophiopogon planiscapus* 'Nigrescens'. Grass.
Strong use of form. Grass is seen as a 'plant' and used as such. For example, the design may have a beautiful Limestone, sinuous pathway, which is flanked on either side by lawns – in this instance the 'green; of the grass is seen as planting, whereas in a Traditional style garden the path is highly likely to be flanked by an herbaceous border on both sides.	Phormiums. Cordylines. *Fatsia japonica*. Yucca's.

Architectural

Architectural planting style is recognizable by its heavy use of strong plant shapes such as columns, cones and fans, which are not softened by the softer mound shapes of grasses and perennials.

Fig. 7.34 Architectural planting style.

Table 7.7 Architectural planting style.

CHARACTERISTICS	KEY PLANTS
Strong form and movement – The movement is seen in the shape of the plant, for example, the strong upright, sword like growth habit of the Phormium tenax family is not dissimilar to that of a firework.	Phormiums. Cordylines. Cardoon. *Yucca gloriosa*. Conifers – for their conical shape.

Chinese/Japanese

The essence of Japanese garden style is of a traditional garden whose design encompasses Japanese aesthetics and philosophical ideas. Artificial ornamentation is frowned upon, and it aspires to highlight the natural landscape.

There are several essential elements of a Japanese garden:

- Water symbolizes renewal, calm, wonder and continuity.
- Stone symbolizes longevity and the forces of nature.
- The Yukimi-gata lantern, or snow lantern, is believed to symbolize the cycle of life, particularly the figure of the mother.
- A bridge is a privileged site for stopping to admire the beauty of the landscape.

The essence of Chinese garden style is based upon two spiritual belief systems: Confucianism and Taoism. Confucianism teaches order and duty, Taoism simplicity and restraint. A Chinese-style garden is very much an outward expression of a culture that embraces these spiritual beliefs, and gives deep insight into the religious culture of two age-old religions.

Fig. 7.35 Kyoto Park Japanese garden.

Table 7.8 Japanese planting style.

CHARACTERISTICS	KEY PLANTS
Very restrained plant palette. Highly ordered, meticulous in their detail and use of materials. Water. Use of rocks. Rocks used to mimic mountains/hillsides in the background.	Acers. Moss. Ferns. Prunus (flowering cherry) trees.

Table 7.9 Japanese dry garden.

CHARACTERISTICS	KEY PLANTS
No plants at all except for the minimal use of moss, perhaps, by the edge of a small pool or at the base of a rock. The Japanese Dry Garden is as it says a dry garden of raked gravel with fourteen, carefully placed rocks. It is a garden intended for deep meditation and contemplation, hence the absence of any plants and colour, which according to the Zen monks, who pioneered this type of garden, would be a distraction.	Moss.

Table 7.10 Chinese planting style.

CHARACTERISTICS	KEY PLANTS
Every element in a Chinese garden has a meaning – even the rocks.	Pinus. Magnolias. Rhododendrons. Dwarf azaleas. Acer trees. Moss. Bamboos. Camellias.
The plant palette is kept to a minimum to accentuate the hard landscaping and structures.	

Scree or GravelGarden

The scree or gravel garden style is particularly appropriate for use in today's unpredictable weather patterns. In a prolonged period of hot, dry summer weather, the tough nature of the plants, together with the

Fig. 7.36 Planting at Beth Chatto's gravel garden in Essex.

Table 7.11 Gravel garden planting style.

CHARACTERISTICS	KEY PLANTS
Drought tolerant plants, in random shaped, smaller manageable groups. Sense of informality. Planting can be walked through and around. Mulched with fine gravel – the gravel serving to reduce surface evaporation from the soil and so, retain moisture. It also serves to provide a hard-wearing surface for walking around the garden, but with no defined pathway.	Grasses. Drought tolerant herbaceous perennials – Echinacea, Kniphofia, *Lychnis coronaria*, Achillea, Acaena 'Blue Haze', Agapanthus, Verbena genus, Verbascums, Sedums, *Stachys byzantina* 'Lamb's Ears', Potentilla, Penstamon,Nepeta,Linum, Limonium, Eryngium, Echinacea. Bulbs – Alliums. Shrubs - Cistus genus and other small shrubs. Perennial Geraniums. Cordylines. Yucca.

gravel mulch, will considerably increase the length of time during which the garden looks colourful and healthy. The nature of the plants – the high density of seed-producing herbaceous perennials and grasses – is a highly valuable resource, providing food for wildlife. Their low maintenance requirements also make this type of garden very desirable for those who have a busy lifestyle. A gravel garden can be created if the slope is shallow; if it is steep, it will need to be reduced by moving soil around and reworking the ground.

Prairie

Prairie-style planting schemes are inspired by the vast, open grasslands of the North American Prairies and include a large number of grasses planted in large swathes punctuated by drifts of colourful perennials. Most of the plants suggested to extend the season of interest in the garden are evergreen and/or provide strong form. They are used to replace the wind-worn trees of the prairies, to provide a second framework that takes over through the winter.

Fig. 7.37 Prairie planting style.

Table 7.12 Prairie planting style.

CHARACTERISTICS	KEY PLANTS
Low usage of shrubs. Late colour - majority of prairie species flower from mid-summer to early autumn, at a time which is often a dull season in many gardens. An extended season of interest provided by the form of some shrubs and conifers in combination with the seedheads of herbaceous flowers and grasses. High percentage of grasses used in drifts. Diverse in both its species and visual content.	Perennials: *Echinacea purpurea*, *Coreopsis grandiflora*, *Monarda fistulosa, Hemerocallis lilioasphodelus*, *Anaphalis margaritacea*, *Nepeta* x *racemosa* 'Superba', *Verbascum chaixii*, *Dianthus carthusianorum*, Sanguisorba, *Verbena hastata*, *Salvia pratensis*, *Geranium 'Johnsons Blue'*, Rudbekia, Helianthemum, Sanguisorba. Grasses: *Deschampsia cespitosa*, *Stipa gigantea*, *Stipa tenuissima*, Pannicum, Calamagrostis, Molinia, Carex, Miscanthus.
	Conifers: *Albertiana conica*, *Albertiana* 'Globe', *Juniper communis* 'Compressa', *Juniper communis* 'Gold Cone', *Juniper horizontalis* 'Glauca', *Juniper horizontalis* 'Lime Glow' , *Juniper scopulorum* 'Blue Arrow', *Cryptomeria japonica*, 'Sekkan Sugi', *Cupressus sempervirens*, *Taxus baccata* 'Fastigiata', *Thuja orientalis* 'Aurea Nana', *Pinus mugo* 'Gnom'.
	Bulbs: Alliums for seedhead interest.
	Plants to Provide an Extended Season of Interest. Shrubs: *Caryopteris* 'Grand Bleu', *Ceratostigma willmottianum*, *Cistus* 'Grayswood Pink', *Cistus* 'Silver Pink', *Cistus* 'Peggy Sammons', *Convolvulus cneorum*, *Cornus alba siberica* *Corokia macrocarpa* 'Red Wonder', *Erysium* 'Bowles Mauve' *Fuchsia* 'Mrs. Popple'.

Colour-Schemed

A colour-schemed or colour-coordinated planting scheme is not conventional in style, but it can produce a striking, highly stylised effect. It is created by using colours only from the same side of the colour wheel. The White Garden at Sissinghurst in Kent is a classic example of a colour-schemed garden.

Fig. 7.38 Colour-schemed planting.

Fig. 7.39 The White Garden at Sissinghurst in Kent.

Plant Use on a Slope

When planting on a slope that remains a slope, and does not have flat terraced areas, there are a number of factors to take into account. For most gardeners, whether amateur or professional, steep banks and slopes pose a challenge, and it cannot be over-emphasized that planting them up with the right plants is key to the success of the entire scheme. Depending upon individual circumstances and preferences, there are several options and the choices you make will depend upon a number of factors:

- Time available for maintenance – a sloping garden takes more energy and effort.
- The level of gardening knowledge – establishing plants on a slope can be complicated, so it is worth keeping it simple at the beginning.
- Budget – choose easy to establish, tough plants.
- How the slope is to be used by the garden owner; is it a single person, a couple or a family?
- Style – if you want a specific style, choose one that uses tough plants that will tolerate challenging conditions or one that replicates a slope in nature, such as a sloping meadow, evergreen conifer slope, a slope planted with fruit trees and meadow grass or a heather-covered bank.
- Speed of coverage required – quick coverage is needed on a slope in order to establish soil stability.

Table 7.13 Common issues when planting on a slope and possible solutions

FACTOR	ISSUE	POSSIBLE SOLUTION	CONSIDERATIONS
Time	Limited time available	Grass	Lawn grass will need more mowing. Meadow grass is wildlife-friendly, needs mowing only twice year, and requires no pesticides/chemicals.
Level of knowledge	Amateur/learner	Use a designer unless on a small site DIY	The designer can plan, cost and organize initial planting and follow up with maintenance support. Extensive research needed. Plants may be lost. Installation and maintenance has to be appropriate for the site. Additional manpower needed for preparation and planting work.
	Knowledgeable	No problems	Work through process of preparation, supplier, establishment, maintenance.
Budget	No limit	Use designer	Employ gardener for maintenance tasks.
	Limited	Use nurseries for plant supply, as this will be cheaper	Need time for establishment care. Select reliable plants.
Use	Single/couple	If garden lovers, no problem	Need time for establishment care. Access needs to be safe for older people. Can be developed over time. Factor in maintenance requirements.
	Family		Access and function need to be safe – no hidden edges on retainers that could cause falls; may need separation with gates, especially if water on lower levels. Need time for establishment care. Slope should be a gentle one. Maintenance – time may be an issue.
Style	Some styles (for example, cottage) are high maintenance	Choose a low-maintenance style	Mix of plants (more architectural style, with evergreens) requires little maintenance. No clipped topiary. Mix of evergreens and flowers is low maintenance.
Coverage of the soil	Soil erosion	Stabilize the soil	Plants with a speedy growth rate – strong-growing climbers or ground-cover plants – will help to stabilize the soil. Ground-cover roses, heathers, red clover, Vinca major, Lamium can be a fast temporary measure.

Once you have looked at the factors that will impact your plant selection, you will be able to take a considered approach to choosing plants for the sloping site. The next step is to look at the choices available.

Table 7.14 Plant choices

REQUIREMENT	ISSUE	POSSIBLE SOLUTION	CONSIDERATIONS
Cover for grassy banks	Safety; may be slippery; especially when wet	Longer neadow grass/wildflower mix	Less formal, naturalistic look. Sow direct on to bare soil. Will need watering and protection from birds. Could use wildflower turf, meadow mat from Environmat or seed-impregnated biodegradable mat.
		Enhance existing grass	Plant up with wildflower plug plants and/or bulbs suitable for naturalizing such as crocus, snowdrops and many narcissus.
Flowers	Maintenance	Low-maintenance perennials	Working on a slope is awkward and uncomfortable, even where it is not steep. It can be made easier by selecting varieties that are drought-tolerant, are self-seeding (and/or spreading), and require little to no pruning or deadheading.
Trees	Will take a while to create cover	Use understorey of shrubs or ground cover	Stabilization of trees and shrubs during establishment phase. Trees will need watering every day while establishing themselves.
Shrubs	Less coverage	Consider buying at larger, semi-mature size	Use membrane and mulch for ground cover during establishment. If the slope is steep, mulch may slip.

Planting design theory is a huge subject, making reference to specific plant characteristics and involving an approach that is very different from thinking about plants merely from the perspective of how to grow them. Once you have a good knowledge of those characteristics, you can use plants to create a specific effect, and the more you do it, the more familiar it becomes. The world of garden design is opened to a bigger, broader world of colour, shape and effect. For example, in a border that is made up mostly of mound-shaped perennial plants, the eye scans over it but fails to pick out anything in particular, unless there is a striking colour. If the same border incorporates a couple of narrow, cone-shaped conifers at either end, and maybe a globe-shaped standard bay tree in the middle, it immediately has much more impact. As an added bonus, it will create an interesting picture, not just in its summer glory but also in winter, as the strong architectural features will appear when all the perennials have died back.

Table 7.15 Plant use: hints and tips

TIPS	REASON
Process	Think: preparation, selection, establishment, maintenance.
Weather	Rain will always cause some soil run-off on a slope, so plant in dry weather.
Use ground cover	Ground-cover plants are one of the best ways to beautify a slope and help prevent erosion. Many are fast-growing, without being invasive.
Reduce maintenance	The initial growth spurt of fast-growing plants will fill a space quickly, but almost all require regular hacking back to look tidy. They can become a pest when they spread to other areas and will increase maintenance work. Select tough plants that are easy to grow and maintain. Right plant, right place – use drought-tolerant plants on a dry slope. On a wet slope, use plants that are tough and will tolerate roots in wet during the winter.
Planting positions	If the slope is up and away from the house, use taller plants towards the middle of the slope and shorter ones towards the bottom of the slope.
Attracting attention	Use plants of the same colour, whether shrubs or perennials, and position them up or down the slope at intervals on the diagonal. This will take the eye either up and across or down and across the slope.
Retaining structures	Walls and timber retaining structures can look hard, so soften them by growing trailing plants – preferably evergreen – to scramble over the edge.
Pocket plants	As the slope goes up or down, there will be pockets and crevices. Plant these with alpines, sempervirens and small trailing plants to create another layer of planting.
Mass planting	A good idea especially when growing to cover large slopes. Choose a variety of plants. One plant en masse can look monotonous and, if a disease or pest attacks, there is a higher chance of the entire area being wiped out and left bare.
Mixed plantings	Disguise small gaps or flaws in the slope.
Trees	Select a mix of evergreen and deciduous, thinking about outline shapes, seasons of interest, eventual heights. If the slope runs away from the property, taller trees will be more visible from the house. Young trees will need staking. May need a barrier in front of the root ball to prevent soil washing away from it.
Shrubs	Use focal-point plants, such as shrubs with variegated or purple foliage, to create 'resting places' for the eye as it works to take in the slope.
Quick impact	Plant some low-growing shrubs or trees for instant impact. Plant clumps of spring-flowering bulbs, such as tulips and daffodils.
Seeding	For a large area, seeding is a good method to cover a lot of ground quickly and cost-effectively. Downsides are that the seeds will need protection from birds, and may give uneven germination, so repeat seeding may be necessary. On a slope, seed may be washed away by heavy rain.
Plan	It is impossible to avoid some soil slippage when planting on a slope. On a small site, it may be minimal, and installation can be achieved in one hit if budget permits. For a large site, draft or sketch a plan divided into areas and cost each area separately, to be actioned as and when time, weather and finances permit.

CHAPTER 8

PLANT GROUPS AND SELECTION

The good news is that once you know which plants will reliably grow and survive on a slope with a reasonable level of maintenance, you can set about planting the garden with confidence. Plant knowledge is hugely beneficial when planning a sloping garden that will thrive, look attractive and help to stabilize the hillside. But where to begin? Trees and shrubs are always reliable and practical plants to use in any garden, but they are especially relevant on a sloping site as their deep and wide root penetration will anchor the soil, while the leafy canopies will reduce the impact of heavy rainfall on the soil surface, protecting the soil underfoot. Quick-growing ground cover will also protect the soil, by reducing surface evaporation and therefore slowing down the speed at which it dries out. Perennial plants will also anchor the soil with their shallow roots, while annuals can be used for quick cost-effective ground cover and colour.

The world of plants can be quite bewildering, so classifying them into groups is useful, as it provides a stronger structure and logical foundation for research and planning. In this chapter, the groups are presented as a small plant library, divided into seven sections, with additional information presented in table format:

- There is a section for each of the main plant groups: trees, conifers, shrubs, perennials, grasses, bulbs and annuals.
- A brief description/definition of each group is given, together with the qualities that each brings to a scheme.
- For each group, there is a list of plants that are considered 'good doers', with images and technical details such as shape, height and width, flowering habit, and so on, for each plant.

When planning a planting scheme, it is normal practice to select the trees, conifers and shrubs first, because they are the structural plants. They form the 'bones' of the garden, on which everything else hangs. When all the summer perennials have died back in autumn, the bare branches of the trees and shrubs will continue to provide interest and beauty with their architectural patterns. Once the type of structural plants has been selected, it is time to think about where they are to be positioned. Decision-making on this can be aided by placing canes upright in the ground where a tree or shrub might go. Step back and assess the balance of height and space; do not forget how much they will grow by the time they reach maturity. Next, the softer hardy perennials, grasses, bulbs and annuals can be chosen, to fill the gaps, add colour and movement and extend the season of interest.

OPPOSITE: Fig. 8.1 Steep planted slope at Kiftsgate Court Gardens in Gloucestershire.

Trees

Trees species range from small, flowering ornamentals suited to the smaller garden to larger parkland/woodland varieties, which are a fabulous feature in a site that has enough space. Trees can be deciduous – losing their leaves in the autumn – or evergreen, and choosing a mix of deciduous and evergreen varieties will provide maximum interest throughout the year. The architectural shapes and winter structure provided by the evergreens and the simple skeletal outlines of deciduous trees will bring interest and pattern to the winter garden. Highlighted with frost and snow in the depths of the winter season, the bare branches will take on a beauty of their own.

When choosing trees, it is important to consider their flowering times. For maximum interest, a tree should be planted for each season: a spring-flowering tree will provide pollen for early bees, summer- and early autumn-flowering trees will extend the food source until the arrival of the cooler temperatures of late autumn, when the garden will benefit from the extra added interest of autumn foliage colour and berries. If space does not allow for three trees, it is possible to select a variety that provides pollen in spring, foliage colour and berries as autumn colour, and a food source for birds and other wildlife.

Table 8.1 Trees

Shape	Single trunk or multi-stemmed Crown can be broad, tall and narrow, conical or weeping
Flowering time	Early spring, summer and autumn, in whites, and various shades of pink
Foliage	Deciduous (lose their leaves in the winter) or evergreen
Foliage colour	Greens and purples through spring and summer. Autumn foliage colour from bright golden yellow to orange to red.
Berries	Some bear fruits such as Malus (crab apple), Crataegus, Sorbus, Amelanchier in autumn.
Texture	Provided by many different bark types, from the smooth deep mahogany of *Prunus serrula* to the glistening white of Betula, to rougher texture of Japanese maple, ash, alder, beech.
Maintenance	Most are low-maintenance Inspect for any diseased/damaged growth in early spring and remove Can be pruned to shape

Table 8.2 Smaller ornamental trees

Amelanchier lamarkii	
Size	Ht: 4–8m. Spread: 4–8m in 10–20 yrs
Soil	Moist/well-drained, acid
Aspect	Full sun and partial shade All directions
Flower	Spring White
Foliage/berries	Deciduous Fantastic yellow/orange autumn foliage colour and deep black/blue berries
Sorbus (mountain ash)	
Size	Ht: 6m. Spread: 3–4m in 10 yrs
Soil	Moist/well-drained, neutral
Aspect	Full sun and partial shade All directions
Flower	Spring White
Foliage/berries	Deciduous Fantastic orange/red autumn foliage colour and red berries
Sorbus aucuparia	
Size	Ht: 6m. Spread: 3–4m in 10 yrs
Soil	Moist/well-drained, neutral
Aspect	Full sun and partial shade All directions
Flower	Spring White
Foliage/berries	Deciduous Fantastic orange/red autumn foliage colour and red berries
Crataegus – several varieties available; 'Paul's Scarlet' is particularly striking	
Size	Ht: up to 6–8m. Spread: 6–8m in 10 yrs
Soil	Any
Aspect	Full sun and partial shade All directions
Flower	Deep pink in spring
Foliage/berries	Deciduous Fantastic orange/red autumn foliage colour and red berries

Fig. 8.2 *Amelanchier lamarckii* 'Ballerina'.

Fig. 8.3 *Crataegus* 'Paul's Scarlet'.

Fig. 8.4 *Betula pendula*.

Table 8.3 Large trees

Betula pendula – white trunk and branches make a stunning feature at night if lit up	
Size	Ht: 5m. Spread: 4m in 10 yrs
Soil	Any
Aspect All directions	Full sun and partial shade
Flower	No flowers, catkins in spring
Foliage/berries	Deciduous
Robinia pseudoacasia 'Frisia'	
Size	Ht: 8–10m Spread: 6–8m in 10 yrs
Soil	Moist/well-drained Will tolerate poor soil
Aspect	Full sun
Flower	Pendant clusters of pea-like flowers
Foliage/berries	Deciduous Yellow/lime in spring maturing to orange/yellow in autumn

LEFT: Fig. 8.5 *Sorbus aucuparia*.

RIGHT: Fig. 8.6 *Robinia pseudoacacia* 'Frisia'.

Conifers

Most conifers are evergreen, except for Larix, which do drop their needles in late autumn. Conifer means 'cone bearer', as conifers produce cones rather than flowers. Their stems are made up of needles or flattened scales rather than leaves.

Table 8.4 Conifers

Shape	Many different shapes, from tall and narrow to conical to rounded. Bring strong, permanent architectural shapes to the scheme. Can be clipped for shape and hedging.
Flowering time	Produce cones rather than flowers
Foliage colour	Vast range of green shades from deep green to bright lime green. Some have a golden colour, some are blue-grey. On some the new growth is a lighter green or it may be variegated.
Texture	Ranges from spiky needles, as in Pinus, Abies and juniper, to softer flattened scale stems of *Thuja orientalis* and Chamaecyparis types
Maintenance	Most are low-maintenance. Inspect for any fungal-type diseases and aphid attack in early spring. Can be clipped to shape.

Table 8.5 Ground-cover conifers with a prostrate growth habit.

Good for permanent ground cover on a slope	
Juniperus squamata	'Blue Carpet'
Size	Ht: 45-60cm. Width: 1.8–2.4m in 7–10 yrs
Soil	Any well-drained soil including chalky and sandy
Aspect	Full sun, dappled shade
Foliage/berries	Cones
Juniperus communis 'Repanda'	
Size	Ht: 45–60cm. Width: 2.5-3m in 7–10 yrs
Soil	Any well-drained soil including chalky and sandy
Aspect	Full sun, dappled shade
Foliage/berries	Blue-grey cones
Juniper procumbens 'Nana'	
Size	Ht: 15–30cm. Width: 1.5–2.5m in 7–10yrs
Soil	Any well-drained soil including chalky and sandy
Aspect	Full sun, dappled shade
Foliage/berries.	Tiny brown/black cones

Fig. 8.7 *Juniperus squamata* 'Blue Carpet'.

Fig. 8.8 *Juniperus communis* 'Repanda'.

Fig. 8.9 *Juniperus procumbens* 'Nana'.

Table 8.6 Conifers with an upright growth habit

Good for adding height on a slope	
Thuja occidentalis 'Smaragd'	
Size	Upright, conical growth habit. Ht: 1.8–2.5m. Width: 60–75cm
Soil	Most soils, but prefers moist, well-drained soil
Aspect	Full sun
Foliage/berries	Small cones
Juniper scopulorum 'Sky Rocket'	
Size	Upright, narrow cone shape. Ht: 2.5–3m. Width: 40–50cm
Soil	Most soils, good drainage
Aspect	Full sun
Foliage/berries	Cones

Fig. 8.10 *Thuja occidentalis* 'Smaragd'.

Fig. 8.11 *Juniperus scopulorum* 'Skyrocket'.

Shrubs

Shrubs are hardy, perennial woody plants. Unlike herbaceous plants, they have a permanent woody framework above the ground all year round. They are good for providing structure, and offer a variety of flowering seasons. Some are scented and roots help to stabilize soil on a slope. They tend to be tough and are relatively easy to grow.

Table 8.7 Shrubs

Shape	Small, medium and large, most are mound-shaped Sizes vary, from 'subshrub', which will grow to approx. 1–1.25m, to larger specimens that can grow to 2–3m.
Flowering time	All seasons
Foliage colour	Usually a range of greens, can be variegated. Most display autumn foliage colour
Berries	Some have berries, such as Pyracantha, Cotoneaster and Berberis.
Texture	Bark and leaves
Maintenance	Most are low maintenance. Once established, they can be pruned to shape after flowering. Check for any damaged diseased wood in early spring and remove. Check for aphid attack. Will benefit from an early spring feed such as pelleted chicken manure. If needed, give a liquid feed as a tonic followed by slow-release granular feed.

Fig. 8.12 *Viburnum tinus*.

Fig. 8.13 *Hypericum forrestii*.

Table 8.8 Evergreen shrubs

Viburnum tinus	
Size	Large mound shape. Ht: 2–3m. Width: 1.8–2.5m in 7–10 yrs Can be used for hedging
Soil	Most soils, moist but well-drained
Aspect	Full sun and light shade
Flower	Clusters of small white flowers in spring/early summer
Foliage/berries	Evergreen, with dark black/blue berries
Hypericum forrestii	
Size	Medium mound shape. Ht: 1.25–1.5m. Width: 1.25–1.5m
Soil	Most soils, well-drained
Aspect	Sun and partial shade
Flower	Bright yellow
Foliage/berries	Dark brown berries
Cotoneaster horizontalis	
Size	Prostrate growth habit. Ht: 80cm–1m. Width: 1.5–1.8m
Soil	Most soils, will tolerate dry conditions
Aspect	Sun/partial shade
Flower	Tiny white flowers in late spring
Foliage/berries	Bright red berries in autumn

Fig. 8.14 *Cotoneaster horizontalis.*

Table 8.9 Deciduous shrubs

Size	Medium-large mound-shape shrub. Ht: 80cm–1.5m. Width: 1m–1.5m
Sambucus nigra 'Black Beauty'	
Size	Large shrub. Ht: 3–4m. Width: 3–4m. Can be hard pruned
Soil	Most soils, humus-rich, well-drained
Aspect	Full sun and partial shade
Flower	Large umbels of tiny white/pink flowers in early summer
Foliage/berries	Clusters of small dark berries in autumn
Cornus 'Midwinter Fire'	
Size	Medium-large mound-shaped shrub. Ht: 80cm–1.5m. Width: 1m–1.5m
Soil	Most soils, prefers moisture
Aspect	Sun and partial shade
Flower	Clusters of small white flowers in spring
Foliage/stems	Fantastic autumn foliage colour. Grown for winter stem colour, which should be pruned back to ground every 2–3yrs, to promote new growth.
Hydrangea quercifolia	
Size	Large mound-shaped shrub. Ht: 1.8–2m. Width: 2–2.5m
Soil	Moist, well-drained, humus-rich
Aspect	Sun and partial shade
Flower	Large cone-shaped clusters of white petals midsummer to autumn
Foliage/berries	Large oak-shaped leaves with red edge. Deep red autumn foliage colour

Fig. 8.15 *Sambucus nigra* 'Black Beauty'.

Fig. 8.16 *Hydrangea quercifolia.*

Fig. 8.17 *Cornus* 'Midwinter Fire'.

Perennials

Perennials are the most versatile of all the plant groups. They grow in all soils, from dry to wet, and in most conditions, from shade to full sun. Most are very easy to grow, quickly filling a border with colour and a variety of heights and leaf shapes. They can be planted in drifts for maximum effect and optimal ground coverage.

Perennials die down below soil level during winter and in the spring start to produce new shoots from the submerged base. They are good on a sloping site because of their shallow root systems, which will quickly stabilize soil and reduce surface evaporation. Many are drought-tolerant, making them ideal for a steep site, where water tends to drain away, and their maintenance requirements are low.

Table 8.10 Perennials

Shape	Various sizes, from ground cover to head-height clumps. Mid-height varieties are mostly mound- and fan-shaped, such as Helenium, Rudbeckia, Echinacea, Persicaria. Taller upright varieties include Veronicastrum, Echium, Helianthus.
Flowering time	Early spring through to autumn, with almost every colour, from white to almost black
Foliage shape and colour	Vast range, from large-leaved hosta to tiny-leaved Veronica Colours are greens, some variegated and some grey/silver In autumn, seed heads can be of interest
Texture	Many different textures, from the spiky flower heads of Eryngium and Echium to the soft feathery flower heads of Sanguisorba
Maintenance	Plants benefit from early spring feed of either pelleted chicken manure, Chempak no.2 for growth followed by Chempak no.4 to promote flowering. Once they have flowered, most can be cut back by 50 per cent to promote second flush flowers. Deadheading also extends the flowering time. Clumps can be split every 3–4 yrs. Seed heads can be left on for winter interest and food source for wildlife. Clumps can be cut back to tidy in spring.
Geranium 'Patricia' ('Brempat')	
Size	Mound shape. Ht: 40–60cm. Width: 80cm–1m
Soil	Most soils
Aspect	Sun and partial shade
Flower	Bright magenta pink with dark centre from early summer–autumn
Foliage/berries	Autumn foliage has red tinge

continued on following page

Table 8.10 continued

Helenium 'Sahins Early Flowerer'	
Size	Medium-height fan-shaped clump. Ht: 50–60cm. Width: 30–40cm
Soil	Most soils
Aspect	Sun and partial shade
Flower	Yellow and terracotta daisy-like flowers
Foliage/berries	Dark brown seed heads in autumn
Monarda 'Cambridge Scarlet'	
Size	Medium-height fan-shaped clump. Ht: 60–70cm. Width: 40–50cm
Soil	Most soils
Aspect	Sun and partial shade
Flower	Scarlet red; Monarda also available in a range of pinks
Foliage/berries	Scented foliage and interesting seed heads for autumn
Rudbeckia 'Goldsturm'	
Size	Medium-height fan-shaped clump. Ht: 50–60cm. Width: 40–50cm
Soil	Most soils
Aspect	Sun and partial shade
Flower	Bright yellow large daisy-like flowers with dark centre
Foliage/berries	Dark seed heads for autumn
Nepeta racemosa 'Walker's Low'	
Size	Medium-height mound-shaped clump. Ht: 40–50cm. Width: 80cm–1m
Soil	Most soils, well-drained
Aspect	Full sun
Flower	Small pale blue flowers from early summer to autumn
Foliage/berries	Pale grey/silver, scented

Fig. 8.18 *Geranium* ‘Patricia’.

Fig 8.19 *Helenium* ‘Sahin’s Early Flowerer’.

Fig. 8.20 *Monarda* 'Cambridge Scarlet'

Fig. 8.21 *Rudbeckia* 'Goldsturm' planted with Echinacea and fennel.

Fig. 8.22 *Nepeta racemosa* 'Walker's Low'.

Perennial Ground-Cover Plants

Ground-cover plants have a flat prostrate growth habit. They are far more attractive to look at than bare earth and can also be grown down wall or rockery faces to soften them. When used on a slope, they protect the topsoil from erosion and drought, and smother weeds, therefore reducing maintenance work.

Table 8.11 Ground-cover plants

Brunnera macrophylla 'Jack Frost'	
Size	Low. Ht: 20–30cm. Width: 40–50cm. Will spread to form drifts
Soil	Moist, well-drained, humus-rich
Aspect	Light to deep shade
Flower	Early spring sprays of forget-me-not blue flowers
Foliage	Deciduous. Fantastic green and silver variegated foliage
Geranium macrorrhizum 'Ingwersens variety'	
Size	Low. Ht: 20–30cm. Width: 30–40cm. Will spread to form drifts
Soil	Moist, well-drained, humus-rich
Aspect	Light to deep shade
Flower	Early spring, white flushed with pale pink flowers
Foliage	Semi-evergreen. Red autumn foliage colour
Lamium maculatum 'Pink Pewter'	
Size	Low. Ht: 2–3cm. Width: 20cm. Will spread to form drifts
Soil	Moist, well-drained, humus-rich
Aspect	Light to deep shade
Flower	Upright stems with small pink flowers, some white varieties also
Foliage	Evergreen. 'Pink Pewter' has green/silver foliage
Vinca major	
Size	Low. Ht: 15–20cm. Width: will spread to form drifts and trail
Soil	Most soils, moist or dry
Aspect	Light to deep shade
Flower	Lilac/blue flowers
Foliage	Evergreen. Deep green foliage

Table 8.11 continued

Persicaria 'Dimity'	
Size	Low. Ht: 20–30cm. Width: will spread to form drifts
Soil	Well-drained, dry
Aspect	Full sun to light shade
Flower	Upright short stems with tiny pink flowers that age to deep rust.
Foliage	Evergreen. Green foliage

TOP LEFT: Fig. 8.23 *Brunnera macrophylla* 'Jack Frost'.
TOP RIGHT: Fig. 8.24 *Geranium macrorrhizum* 'Ingwersens Variety'.
LEFT: Fig. 8.25 *Vinca major*
BOTTOM LEFT: Fig. 8.26 *Lamium maculatum* 'Pink Pewter'.
BOTTOM RIGHT: Fig. 8.27 *Persicaria* 'Dimity'.

Climbing Plants as Ground Cover

Climbing plants are usually used for their upward growth habit, but they can also be planted and left to sprawl over the ground, very successfully covering the soil with foliage and flower. A stem in contact with the soil surface will also root and soon produce a new plant. Clematis do this with ease and ground-cover clematis have recently been bred purely for this purpose. *Clematis* recta is a great example of this.

Roses for Ground Cover

Roses have been less popular of late, but they can be used for high-impact mass plantings. The vigorous growth of low-growing ground-cover roses, such as the single white Rosa 'Partridge', will very quickly provide foliage cover and summer flowers to a slope. There are other colours available.

Rosa rugosa types have a vigorous, bushy growth habit with large single white or pink flowers during the summer. Marble-sized orange hips provide autumn colour. Mass plantings look very attractive and are also an excellent food source for pollinators and wildlife.

Fig. 8.28 *Clematis* recta.

Fig 8.29 *Rosa* 'Partridge' is a good ground-cover rose.

Fig. 8.30 *Rosa rugosa* 'Alba' has large hips for autumn interest.

Grasses

Grasses are part of the perennial family. Most are deciduous, but still provide wonderful creamy, buff foliage colour and numerous delicate seed heads, which provide autumn interest as well as a great food source for winter wildlife. There are also some evergreen varieties, such as *Stipa gigantea* with its evergreen base and Anemanthele lessoniana. Both of these provide mid-height greenery for the winter months.

Grasses have a shallow root system that will quickly stabilize soil and reduce surface evaporation on a slope. Most are easy to grow. They should be planted in drifts for maximum effect and ground coverage on a slope. Maintenance requirements are low – deciduous types simply need cutting back to approximately 200mm in January or February. Many are drought-tolerant, making them the ideal plant for a steep slope where water tends to drain away.

Table 8.12 Grasses

Shape	Varies from tall and narrow, to mound- and fan-shaped
Flowering time	Early summer through to late summer/early autumn
Foliage colour	Mostly green; some have orange colouration and some variegated
Texture	Most look soft and feathery and all provide movement
Stipa gigantea	
Size	Tall. Ht: 1.8–2m. Width: 70–90cm
Soil	Moderately fertile, medium to light well-drained
Aspect	Full sun
Flower	Late spring to autumn
Foliage	Evergreen base of narrow arching leaves
Molinia caerulea subsp. arundinacea 'Transparent'	
Size	Tall. Ht: 1.8–2m. Width: 70–90cm
Soil	Moderately fertile, medium to light well-drained
Aspect	Full sun and light shade
Flower	July to autumn Great self-seeder
Foliage	Delicate flower heads with tiny, beaded seed heads

ABOVE LEFT: Fig. 8.31 *Stipa gigantea,* otherwise known as 'Golden Oats'.

ABOVE RIGHT: Fig 8.32 *Molinia caerulea subsp. arundinacea* 'Transparent'.

BELOW LEFT: Fig 8.33 *Calamagrostis* 'Karl Foester' planted behind yellow Rudbeckia.

BELOW RIGHT: Fig 8.35 Calamagrostis brachytricha.

Table 8.12 continued

Calamagrostis 'Karl Foester'	
Size	Medium. Upright growth habit. Ht: 1.2–1.4m. Width: 30–40cm
Soil	Moist, humus-rich
Aspect	Full sun and light shade
Flower	June to autumn. Long narrow cream flower heads
Foliage	Narrow arching green leaves *Calamagrostis* 'Overdam' has variegated foliage
Stipa tenuissima	
Size	Small. Ht: 30–40cm. Width: 20–30cm
Soil	Moderately fertile, medium to light well-drained
Aspect	Full sun and light shade
Flower	Soft, feathery flower heads from early summer Great self-seeder
Foliage	Narrow, semi-evergreen base Develops some cream/buff colour through winter
Calamagrostis brachytricha	
Size	Medium. Ht: 80cm–1m. Width: 50–60cm
Soil	Moist, humus-rich
Aspect	Full sun and light shade
Flower	Soft, silvery flower heads in late summer
Foliage	Upright, green leaves

Fig 8.34 *Stipa tenuissima* and a fan palm.

Bulbs

A bulb is a rounded underground structure not unlike an onion when cut in two. From the small snowdrop and crocus to larger Narcissus varieties, Tulips and Alliums, bulbs can provide colour in all the seasons. All produce leaves and flower from the centre of the bulb. They are good for slope planting as they can be left in situ once they have been planted, and the root mat of established clumps will provide stabilization of the soil. They have low maintenance requirements, although clumps may need splitting every 4 to 5 years. They should be used in conjunction with other planting as they die back below the ground once they have flowered.

Fig. 8.36 *Crocosmia masoniorum*.

Fig. 8.37 *Narcissus* 'Tête-à-Tête'.

Fig. 8.38 *Eranthis hyemalis*.

Fig. 8.39 *Allium hollandicum* 'Purple Sensation'.

Table 8.13 Bulbs

Shape	Huge range of flower shapes, depending on variety
Flowering time	From late winter to late autumn
Foliage colour	From grey/green to bright green
Crocosmia masoniorum	
Size	Medium. Ht: 40–45cm
Soil	Well-drained, humus-rich
Aspect	Full sun and light shade
Flower	July to August
Foliage	Deciduous. Bright green strappy foliage
Narcissus 'Tête-à-Tête'	
Size	Small. Ht: 25–30cm. Width: 20–30cm. Will spread to form a drift
Soil	Well-drained, humus-rich
Aspect	Full sun and light shade
Flower	Late winter/early spring (Jan/Feb)
Foliage	Deciduous. Bright green strappy foliage
Eranthis hyemalis	
Size	Low. Ht: 2–3cm. Width: 20–30cm. Will spread to form a drift
Soil	Well-drained, humus-rich
Aspect	Full sun and light shade
Flower	Late winter/early spring (Jan/Feb)
Foliage	Deciduous. Green, petal-shaped leaves around the flower
Allium hollandicum 'Purple Sensation'	
Size	Medium. Ht: 30–40cm. Width: 30–40cm
Soil	Well-drained, humus-rich
Aspect	Full sun and light shade
Flower	Large, rounded, purple, umbellifer shape from late May for 2–3 weeks
Foliage	Deciduous. Wide, strappy pale green leaves

Annuals

An annual is a plant that completes its life cycle, from germination to the production of seeds, within one growing season, and then dies.

Annuals are used for quick cover and flower colour in the garden. Meadow-type annuals such as cornflowers, poppies and ox-eye daisies will self-seed, so once sown they should repeat flower every year from new flushes of seedlings. Varieties such as Phacelia and red clover, known as 'green manure', are particularly beneficial for fixing nitrogen in the soil thereby improving its nutritional values.

Annuals are relatively easy to grow from seed, in a greenhouse or on a warm windowsill. Sowing instructions and timings for each type are on the packet. On very free-draining soil, it can be possible to sow and grow them outside. October/November is the optimal time to sow annuals into open ground, to give them an opportunity to germinate and make seedlings, which will over-winter and then continue to grow the following spring. They will flower through from May or June, when they can be cut back and left to decompose on the soil surface or dug into the soil.

Fig. 8.40 *Erigeron karvinkskianus* planted with prostrate rosemary, a fantastic ground-cover plant.

Table 8.14 Annuals

Shape	Wide variety of shape, from low to tall, narrow and sprawling
Flowering time	Mostly summer-flowering; huge range of colour

Table 8.15 Best annuals

Easy-to-grow annuals for summer flower in sun (excluding bedding plants). Sow as per sowing instructions on the packet.	
Cornflower	Blue or pink Grows to approx. 300mm in height
Eschscholzia (Californian poppy)	Yellow, orange, white or pink Grows to approx. 300mm in height
Cosmos	White, pale pink, deep pink or pink and white Grows to approx. 600mm in height
Nigella and Cerinthe.	Both grow to approx. 300mm
Cleome	Pink or white Grows to approx. 600–900mm in height

Planting Tips

Self-Seeders

Self-seeders can be used to fill any gaps with fast growth, and will provide repeat flowering every year at minimal cost. Some of the best to try are the following:

- compact sweet Alyssum;
- creeping Phlox;
- small Alpine plants;
- creeping thyme;
- Sedum and Sempervivum varieties.

Fig. 8.41 Sweet Alyssum.

A sloping garden that has rocks, steps or retaining walls will have lots of nooks and crannies that offer the opportunity to plant self-seeding plants, which will soon grow and start to provide cover. As self-seeders, they are an extremely cost-effective way to create some quick ground cover which will repeat year on year.

Small alpine plants will thrive in the crevices between stones and rocks. They are tough plants that demand little care and attention, and many are evergreen. Stems in contact with the soil surface will root and create new plants, so over time they can provide extensive ground cover. For maximum impact, choose plants with contrasting foliage shape and colour.

Fig. 8.42 Creeping Phlox.

Drought Resistance

For balance, medium-height drought-resistant plants, such as Lavender, Santolina and Phormium, can be underplanted with a low layer of ground covers and succulents. All these plants will tolerate several weeks without water and aid in the prevention of erosion, a natural hazard of all gardens on a slope.

Fig. 8.43 Creeping thyme.

Fig. 8.44 *Thymus turkestanica* is great for ground cover.

Fig. 8.45 Sempervivum.

Fig. 8.46 Sedum.

Fig. 8.47 Planting by a path at the top of a slope.

Growing Zones

All selected plants need to be appropriate for the growing zone of the site, and the level of frost that can be expected in the area. If the slope is exposed to high winds, the garden will need tough plants that are resistant to their drying effects. A low hedge may be planted to act as a wind barrier to protect the plants within its boundaries. Acers will suffer from leaf browning and loss if exposed to wind.

Timescale

When developing a large sloping site, it is a good idea to divide the planting into phases. Tackling the task over time reduces the financial impact and will allow you to get to know the site well. Over the months and years, trees and shrubs will become large structural plants, so their position is key to the scheme looking right. That insignificant 30-cm shrub from the nursery could become a 2-metre giant in 7 to 10 years, and end up blocking up that lovely view! Fillers – perennials and grasses – can be mass planted in large drifts to create a high-impact meadow or prairie effect, taking into account the need for some follow-on interest when they die down in autumn.

Fig. 8.49 Nigella and Cerinthe.

Fig. 8.48 Eschscholzia.

Stabilization

Overall, the main aim when planting a slope is first to eradicate soil erosion. If the slope is steep and funds do not allow for the creation of flat terraces, then planting is the way forward to create a stable, attractive slope.

The View

A slope that runs uphill away from the house will act as a stage for the plants, as they will all be seen from the property. Remember when planting trees and shrubs that the taller they get the taller they will seem as the upward slope increases their height.

Where a slope runs downhill away from the house, the design will need to provide an intriguing entrance or access to entice people into the garden, or a pathway that runs along the top so that the view is from above. Taller plant shapes will at first only just poke their head above the patio edge or may not be seen at all unless they are planted at the top of the slope.

Watering

On a newly planted slope, it is important to carry out watering at regular intervals, whether it is a hot, dry slope or a cooler, shady site. Trees and shrubs will need to be watered daily, unless the weather is wet, until new growth emerges, signalling that the plant has established a good root system and can sustain its own water supply. During periods of hot, dry weather, it will be necessary to take a regular walk around the garden to inspect plants for drying leaves and wilting stems, which will indicate that additional watering is required. Watering at the base of the plant so that the root ball gets a good soak is far more effective than sprinkling over the top. Even when drought-tolerant plants have been chosen, they can still suffer when newly planted.

Applying a mulch such as chipped tree bark, compost or grass clippings will slow down surface evaporation, help to conserve moisture in the soil and provide nutrition as it breaks down.

Developing a knowledge of plants, how they are categorized into specific groups, their characteristics and maintenance requirements and what they will bring to a planting scheme, will go a long way to the development of a successful scheme. The plants recommended here have a toughness that makes them ideal for the unique challenges of a garden on a slope. They are easy to establish and, as long as the correct early care is given, should pose very few problems to the gardener, whether keen, professional or novice.

Plants are the living element of a garden and should be chosen for their suitability to the specific environment. Following this basic advice is a key ingredient for success and should result in a healthy, thriving sloping garden that is a joy to look at.

Fig. 8.50 The planting process.

CONCLUSION

A garden, whether flat or sloping, is a place for outdoor entertainment or physical activity, or simply an outdoor room for sitting and relaxing. It can also take on the extended role of home office or a much-needed 'green therapy room' that will re-energize and uplift the garden owner and their visitors.

The picture that a sloping garden presents is visually more interesting than that of a flat one. Its changing levels draw the eye in as the observer seeks to understand them. Indeed, many owners with flat gardens seek to introduce changes of level. Developing a sloping garden poses a challenge that may be daunting but it will be made more manageable when you are armed with the right information. From assessing the slope and creating a brief or plan of action to the final stages of plant selection and planting, using the methods recommended here is the best way to achieve a successful outcome.

The life of the garden owner is intertwined with that of their garden, and the life of the garden is governed by the seasons. Often, it is buying a house with a garden in poor condition, or a sloping garden, that is the trigger for the non-gardener to discover a new interest.

Whether it is large or small, the completion of a garden project gives a great sense of satisfaction, and that sense will continue to be felt year after year as the garden develops. A successful sloping garden is not just about the planting; the changing levels provide a stage for dressing with plants, making for an intriguing garden journey, whether up or down.

Inevitably, a garden will change from year to year, as plants increase in size, and their impact within the planting scheme alters. Indeed, this is one of the great things about gardens and plants – nothing remains static. As the garden is enjoyed and observed over time, anything organic that does not seem quite right can be changed – plants can be removed, moved or replaced. Inevitably, the more a project has been planned beforehand, the more likely it is that it will look right, and this is especially the case when working with a sloping garden.

There are few books that focus on the sloping garden. The information in this one is based on both my personal experience of designing and constructing sloping gardens, and of working on my own garden, which is on three different levels. Whether you are a garden owner, student or professional, it can be used for advice and guidance or maybe just reassurance, while developing or designing your own version. If you explore it to the full, a sloping garden that has excellent functionality and looks beautiful can be yours to enjoy for many years to come.

RECOMMENDED GARDENS AND NURSERIES

Gardens

Westbury Court Garden, Westbury-on-Severn, Glos GL14 1PD Tel: 01452 760461

Mount Stewart Garden, County Down, N. Ireland BT24 7LH

Kiftsgate Garden, Chipping Campden, Gloucestershire GL55 6LW Tel: 01386 438777

Knoll Gardens, Wimborne, Dorset BH21 7ND Tel: 01202 873931

Sezincote Garden, Moreton-in-Marsh, Gloucestershire GL56 9AW

The Trentham Estate, Stone Road, Trentham, Stoke-on-Trent ST4 8JG Tel: 01782 646646

Painswick Rococo Garden, Painswick, Gloucestershire GL6 6TH Tel: 01452 813204

Hampton Court Castle, Leominster, Herefordshire HR6 0PN Tel: 01586 797777

Abbotsbury Garden, Weymouth, Dorset DT3 4LA Tel: 01305 871387

The Lost Gardens of Heligan. St Austell, Cornwall PL26 6EN Tel: 01726 845100

The Eden Project, St Austell, Cornwall PL24 2SG Tel: 01726 811911

RHS Rosemoor Garden, Devon EX38 8PH Tel: 01805 624067

Compton Acres, Poole, Dorset BH13 7ES Tel: 01202 700778

Burford House, Tenbury Wells, WR15 8HQ Tel: 01584 810777

Beth Chatto Gardens, Colchester, Essex CO7 7DB Tel: 01206 822007

Winterbourne Botanic Garden, Edgbaston, Birmingham B15 2RT Tel: 0121 414 3832

Nurseries

Knoll Garden Nurseries, Wimborne, Dorset BH21 7ND Tel: 01202 873931

Badger Nurseries, Mappleborough Green, Warwickshire B80 7DL Tel: 01527 852631

Cotswold Garden Flowers, Badsey, Worcestershire WR11 7EZ Tel: 01386 833849

Hardy's Cottage Garden Plants, Whitchurch, Hampshire RG28 7FA
Tel: 01256 896533 info@hardysplants.co.uk

INDEX

Plant index